THERE IS NO BLACK OR WHITE

Eric F. Legge

iUniverse, Inc.
Bloomington

There Is No Black Or White

Copyright © 2011 Eric F. Legge

iUniverse books may be ordered through booksellers or by contacting:

iUniverse
1663 Liberty Drive
Bloomington, IN 47403
www.iuniverse.com
1-800-Authors (1-800-288-4677)

ISBN: 978-1-4620-2059-1 (sc)
ISBN: 978-1-4620-2060-7 (e)

Printed in the United States of America

iUniverse rev. date: 5/10/2011

This book is dedicated to those who did not come home. It is also dedicated to the families who now must live without them. It was not in vain.

QUOTES

Col. Burdine: Extremely brave. Always wanted to do what was right. He not only talked the talk, but walked the walk.

Extraordinary man and soldier. He's the kind of soldier that makes it all worthwhile.

General Gossell: Captain Legge is a fine Marine who I would be honored to serve with.

Lt. Col. Bacon: Eric saved lives, averaging a Marine a week by being the catalyst that restored a hotline…

FORWARD

I originally started writing the stories that follow for two reasons. The first was therapeutic. I wanted to get some of the things I had gone through down on paper so that I could reflect on what I am certain will be one of the most interesting years I have spent thus far. The second was for my family. I wanted to give them something back for the year that they had to endure back at home.

If you are looking for a military book that tells of great heroics and non-stop action that is rife with firefights, this book is not for you. I never fired a single shot during my tour in Iraq. The closest I ever came to shooting anyone was a six-foot tall woman who showed up at one of our town hall meetings in a very dangerous part of Ramadi. She wore a burqa so completely enveloping that even her eyes were masked. Her gloved hands looked twice as large as mine, and they kept fidgeting with her purse. I was certain she was a man, and was on a suicide mission. I had my 9mm pistol out in my lap for twenty minutes, loaded, cocked, and ready to shoot this woman in the temple. The Marines who were in charge of security had thoroughly screened her. They sat in the back of the room laughing for twenty minutes.

I have really tried to only stick with the facts throughout the first thirty-one chapters. I have tried to recall certain missions that I went on and things that happened during my time in Iraq, and not my opinion of what transpired. The last chapter of this book is my opinions on how I felt. I highly recommend that you read the first thirty chapters and ignore the last chapter. One thing I have learned in my years on this earth, some people take their own opinions way too seriously.

This tendency causes men and women to die on the battlefield, and it has since the beginning of time. Just a bit of tolerance and respect for others opinions would reduce this bloodshed beyond everyone's wildest imagination. It would not eliminate war. War and violence are just as much a part of life as breathing. I hate to say that and wish with all my heart it were not true, but as a soldier, it is simply something we have to face.

This book is written not only for my family but for those families that gave the ultimate sacrifice by losing a loved one. My thanks go out to them, and I wanted you to see some of the things that go on in war that rarely come to light. I am proud of my contribution to something that will probably not become defined in history for many more years to come. To have been among those brave soldiers is something I will always cherish and will never forget.

CHAPTER ONE

MARCH 2005
FORT WORTH, TEXAS

I was sworn into the Marine Corps for the second time on March 10, 2005 as the "oldest Lieutenant in the history of the Marine Corps," according to Major General William Gossell. At the small but meaningful ceremony, I recall asking Gen. Gossell if I could have the title of the most handsome Lt. in the Corps, rather than the oldest, but was informed by the General that he had been given that title some forty years ago. The title seemed harmless, and I am certain that it is not true, but it seemed to stick with me and would follow me to the halls of the American Embassy in Baghdad.

I took the oath in March of 2005 and by May was put on active duty in Charlotte, NC. Col. Paul Brier was charged with the task of starting up a brand new Civil Affairs Group to relieve 5th and 3rd CAG from having to do back-to-back tours. We were to be 6th CAG, designed to be a unit for only one year, then to be disbanded and never to be used again.

Charlotte was just the staging ground for setting up the logistics of the CAG; it would not be activated until June. I was there a month early to see if there was anything I could do to help. For the first month, I think I was more of a hindrance than a help, but I was getting acclimated to being in uniform and taking orders again. You would be surprised how quickly you snap back into taking orders. There were only around ten Marines in Charlotte preparing to start up a unit of around 190 Marines. On June 1st, we packed up our gear and headed to Camp Lejeune in Jacksonville, North Carolina.

6th CAG sign out front of the Command Center,
Camp Blue Diamond, Ramadi, Iraq.

Camp Lejeune is one of the largest Marine bases in the world. Maybe not in size, but as far as the population of grunts, there is nowhere that has more. It is where the ground pounders train, rather than pilots or other MOS's (Military Occupation Specialty) in the Marine Corps. It is, therefore, just by the nature of things, the highest concentration per square foot of testosterone in the universe. It was good to be back, but I was soon to find out what it took to be a Marine again.

One of the first things that make the Marine Corps who they are is what we affectionately called "five o'clock at the pull-up bars." Every morning at 0500, we met at the pull-up bars in front of French Creek quarters to begin our morning exercises. Now for you civilians, who I had been just a few precious weeks prior, 5:00 in the morning does not really mean 5:00 in the morning. In fact, no time in the Marine Corps really means the time that is stated. It means 0445 in the morning. If you have a meeting at 10:00 in the morning, it means you have to be there at 9:45. This was one of the hardest lessons I had to get used to being in the Corps.

Months later, I would be close to getting killed by one of our Lt. Col.'s in Baghdad when I slept in just a little too long and was not out in front of my hooch at 0745 for what he had told me was 0800. He yelled and yelled

2

at me, swearing he was going to shoot me if I was ever late again, until he finally couldn't help but laugh uncontrollably at what he knew would never be a squared-away Marine.

It was not for lack of trying. I swear, I really tried to get the hang of being fifteen minutes or thirty minutes early to every meeting, depending on the rank of the officer setting the time, but I have to admit I never really did get the hang of it. For those Marines who were below me, and there were not many, I told them over and over again that when I set a time for a meeting, I expected them to be in formation, toes on the line, exactly when I set the meeting. If they wanted to be there fifteen minutes early, losing fifteen minutes of sleep, that was their doing, not mine.

CHAPTER TWO

OCTOBER 1983
NORMAN, OKLAHOMA

When I first joined the United States Marine Corps in 1983, I had just graduated from the University of Oklahoma, was already married and had a six-month-old baby girl. I've often been asked why I joined the Marine Corps in the first place. I am not sure any Marine can actually tell you why they made the auspicious decision to join the United States Marine Corps. My father-in-law had a career in the United States Air Force, retiring as a Lt Col. I can recall him telling hundreds of stories about the escapades he and his wife had been through all over the world. They left their mark in Officer's Clubs from Montana to Japan. The fond memories they recalled and the exciting life of living abroad sounded intoxicating. I had worked my way through college, working on various golf courses in the Oklahoma City area and the excitement of being a pilot and seeing the world seemed to be exactly what I needed.

As it is in any college town, military recruiters have offices that are clearly visible near the student lounge. I had passed the Air Force recruitment office hundreds of times, so one day I got enough guts to walk in and see what they had to offer. For those who have never actually talked to a military recruiter, it is very much like buying a used car. They're always smiling and they will say whatever they think you want to hear in order to get you in that car. I heard stories of how great the United States Air Force was, all the adventures that I was going to have over the next 20 years, and how at the age of 42, I was going to be able to retire and never have to work another day in my life. It was what I wanted to hear, and I was ready to sign up.

The only problem, at the time, was they only had two slots open for pilots in the Air Force in my district. There were over 200 applicants for these two slots. My grades in college were not exactly stellar, to say the least. Needless to say, I was not one of the two selected. Looking back on it, I'm sure that the recruiter, who took my application, went directly to the Marine Corps recruiting office right next door and said, "In two weeks I'll have a new recruit for you."

When the results came in, the recruiter was kind enough to call and ask me to come down to his office to get the results of my application. Upon arriving, I was curious why there was a well-dressed Marine in that unmistakable recruiting uniform they wear. When I walked in the office, he looked at me like a lion ready for his next meal. The Air Force recruiter shook my hand, thanked me for putting in my application, but gave me the sad news that only two people were accepted in the entire district. He then turned to the Marine Corps recruiter, introduced me and said the Marines were always looking for a few good men. At the time I had my hopes set very high on being a pilot. The movie "An Officer and a Gentleman" had just come out, and I was looking for a future. In hindsight, it turned out to be a very good thing that I knew little to nothing about the United States Marine Corps.

As I recall, the Marine Corps was not the easiest branch to get into, let alone being guaranteed a shot at becoming a pilot. I needed a letter of recommendation from my congressman to get in, but I was finally accepted. I was given a date of December 17, 1983 when I would officially belong to the Marine Corps. This meant that not only was I going to miss Christmas, but I would also not be home for my child's first birthday. As I prepared for the 17th, somehow things changed without any notice. I was contacted on the 16th and told that a van would pick me up and take me to a nearby hotel so that I would be ready for the flight to Quantico the next day. What was I to say? "No thanks Sarge. I'll just see you at the airport?"

My recruiter had been very open with me about what to expect once the Marine Corps got their hands on me. The first two weeks of Officer Candidate School (OCS) was going to be tough. It would be physically demanding, as well as, emotionally stressful. But after the first two weeks you "get the weekends off," and they start treating you like a human being again. Any other Marines out there get to go to this OCS school? I think they sent me to the wrong place.

I don't think it is possible to explain what boot camp is really like. Forgive the analogy, and I am sure this will offend 51 percent of the population, but it is much like a man saying he knows what it is like to have a baby. I am not actually comparing labor to boot camp… unless labor lasts twelve weeks. Major Tracy commanded the OCS class that I was lucky enough to go through. He was a Mustang Marine, which meant that although he was an officer, he had come up through the enlisted ranks. Although I have not seen him in over twenty-five years, I can still see those steely gray eyes that could burn a hole right through your head if you made the mistake of getting his full attention.

The secret to getting through boot camp is not drawing attention to oneself. If your drill instructor had a tough time remembering your name, you were just where you wanted to be. This was not the situation for me. My drill instructors, Staff Sgt. Gerrard and Sgt. Lynch not only knew my name right away, but somehow I ended up being known by the drill instructors in the four other platoons as well. This was not a good thing.

I was always the class clown in my school days. Cracking jokes at the least opportune times. My principals all knew me by name. Now my drill instructors were becoming much too familiar with me as well. One of the hardest things to explain to someone who has not gone through Marine Corps boot camp is that you cannot take a piss without someone yelling behind you. The overbearing presence of a drill instructor is there all day long. When you finally get to hit the rack after polishing your boots and getting all your gear ready for the next day, and maybe writing a quick letter home, you would think we would be able to rest because the drill instructors had to sleep as well.

I have never been a drill instructor, and I don't know this for a fact, but I don't think they sleep.

As soon as they have made their rounds several times after lights out, yelling at those who got caught polishing their boots in the dark (boots were somehow supposed to magically end up polished the next morning), they retreated into their drill instructor caves, which we were never allowed to enter, and stayed up all night planning what horrible things they were going to do to the candidates the next day. We, in the meantime, all slept with one eye open so that the fifty gallon aluminum trash can that was going to be tossed on the concrete floors of our barracks at 4:30 in the morning, sounding the alarm for another fun day, would not wake us from a dead sleep.

The first two weeks went by, and I swear I was still expecting what my recruiter had said about the weekends off to come true. What actually happened was that on the third weekend they dangled that chance of getting some liberty if we all passed inspection. "Inspection" meant having everything on you/around you/not around you being clean/polished/put away. In other words everything had to be plain old perfect. It is a lot like trying to have two hundred kids at Chuck E. Cheese totally silent and still for an hour. In our case, we would have to stand at attention for hours, waiting on the commanding officer to come to our quarters to see if any of our shaved heads had one hair pointing in the wrong direction.

The Saturday of the third weekend went by, and I am fortunate enough to be among the only company in OCS history to have been so screwed up that they were considering changing all of our status to the Army. We were instructed to re-clean, re-polish, re-do everything that we had screwed up in the first place. Then maybe, just maybe, we would get liberty on Sunday.

We spent all night trying to unscrew ourselves. Sunday was the same routine. Stand at attention hour after hour, with the occasional candidate falling over backwards because he lost the circulation in his lower legs. It goes without saying; we did not receive that elusive liberty pass. The next Saturday, same thing. Sunday, no different. Another weekend lost. Next Saturday and Sunday, same routine. We were coming into the sixth week of training and were all ready to go crazy. By then we had hardened up both physically and mentally, but were all close to snapping. My snap was to come after liberty.

The Marine Corps is by far hardest on the families of the Marine. Whether they are in boot camp or at war, family members are helpless with regard to what happens to their Marine. My wife was no exception. We had our first child six months before I had finished what seemed like eleven years to get my under graduate degree. Then to have to handle our daughter's first Christmas and first birthday alone was, to say the least, stressful. Her helplessness turned into fear. She was certain that I was either dead or kidnapped. During one of our inspections, while standing at attention, a messenger was sent to our brand new barracks saying that I had an emergency phone call. This was the first and last time that situation happened in our company. We had been moved from what was called the white elephant, a building that had been built before fire was invented, to brand new barracks.

The problem with the new barracks was they were not fully completed. What was missing was the lifeline between a Marine and his loved ones. A phone. Whenever we were given the opportunity to make a call, we had to run around three fourths of a mile to a small exchange where we could buy candy, which at the time was called poguey bait. I have no idea why.

Out in front of the exchange, nearly always in the rain, was a single pay phone. Normally, we had to stand in line for hours waiting on the Marines ahead of us, hanging onto every word of the family members that spoke from the real world so far away.

Due to the fact everyone was in formation when I received the call, my run to the phone ended with no line to wait in. I was hesitant to make the call, because whatever was at the other end of the line was important enough to convince some of the most hardened Marines to let me make the call. I called home expecting the worst. My wife answered the phone.

"Is everything OK?" was all I could say.

My wife started crying, and all I can really remember her saying was that she just had to hear my voice. She was certain that something had happened to me. It was around the fourth week at the time and we had very little chance to make phone calls. After asking her at least twenty times if she was certain that nothing was wrong and telling her at least forty times that I was fine, she said she just had to see me in person to put her mind at ease.

At the time, the occasional meal at McDonald's was a complete luxury to us. For her to fly out to Washington just to see me during my theoretical "liberty" seemed to be ridiculous, but she was adamant. I told her that liberty was completely uncertain, but talk was going around that they had to let us go eventually, so I told her to get a ticket for the fifth weekend. Surely we would be given a break by then. I told her to get a room at the Marriott in Crystal City and just hope that I managed to get there.

The next weekend came with the same results. No liberty. The following week I was lucky enough to have a company billet. I was the candidate Gunnery Sergeant. There were four company billets given to four of the luckiest candidates each week where each candidate had to follow the actual Gunnery Sergeant, First Sergeant, Executive Officer, or Commanding Officer. This was no honor. This was torture. You were put under the spotlight and spent a week of pure hell.

As the candidate gunny, I had to do everything. Gunnies are the heart of the Marine Corps and do what seems like 90 percent of the work. Twenty-five years later, while in Iraq, some of the finest men I have ever met were Gunnies. The gunny in boot camp was no exception, although I can't remember his name. I think I have blocked it out, because being a good Marine in a training position meant to inflict as much pain, pressure, and torture to his trainees as is humanly possible. This gunny was good.

He had me running around like a chicken with its head cut off. He would tell me to get this or that, I would run across the base to get it only to come back knowing what to expect.

"Candidate Legge, for Christ sake, can't you do anything right! That is not what I asked for!"

He derived such pleasure in trying to humiliate me in front of his peers, the other drill instructors. He even gave me a very special name. Again, I apologize for not remembering the exact name. I swore that I would never forget it.

At the time I knew nothing of the significance of the name. The gunny just told me that whenever he asked me my name, I was to shout out "Candidate Williams." I know it was not Williams, but you get the idea. Every time another drill instructor was anywhere in the vicinity, the gunny would say, "Hey, you gotta watch this." He would turn to me with that wry smile and say, "Candidate, what's your name?"

I would stand at attention and yell out, "Candidate Williams."

"Where you from?" he would shout back.

"George Washington Academy, Gunnery Sergeant."

The drill instructor nearby would just break out laughing. I guess I just did not understand real Marines' sense of humor. I am not sure exactly when I found out the meaning of "Candidate Williams," but the down and dirty of it was that some kid named Williams was kicked out of a military school because they found out he was gay. I guess it made the papers; so all the drill instructors just thought this was a hoot.

The rest of my stay at OCS was accompanied with every drill instructor in the place, every time they saw me... "Candidate! What's your name?"

"Candidate Williams!"

"Where you from?"

"George Washington Academy!" I would scream at the top of my lungs.

As a matter of fact, the more they did it, the louder I got. We would be running through the hills of Quantico, filled with trees and virtually no visibility and all you would hear was some drill instructor yell, "What's your name!" Although there were two hundred and fifty of us running, I knew who they were yelling at. I never once failed to send back my response as loud as I could muster.

The week before my wife was to come to DC was pure hell. They had pushed me to the absolute limit of my endurance. I was even called into my drill instructor's office so he could give me a talking to. I think they were getting a little pissed off at the defiance in my voice every time one of them called out, "What's your name?" This was supposed to be humiliating to me but was turning into what might appear as me mocking them. I was.

"Candidate Legge, what is your problem?" asked Staff Sgt Gerrard.

SSgt. Gerrard was a very trim, very fit, southern gentleman that to this day, I consider to be one of the finest I have met in the Corps. He was absolutely hard core, yelled at you all the time, but you could tell it was out of his professionalism that made him do the things he did. You could tell he was doing his job, not getting some sadistic pleasure out of it like some of the other drill instructors.

"The Candidate has no problem Drill Instructor," was my reply.

He repeated the question, this time with much more authority.

"What's your problem Candidate Legge?!"

I could tell he was pissed, but I did not know what he wanted of me, so I repeated,

"The Candidate has no problem, Drill Instructor."

He was getting more pissed.

"You think you're a tough guy, don't you Candidate!" yelled SSgt. Gerrard, a half an inch away from my face. I could feel the heat of his anger on my face.

"The Candidate thought that is what you wanted out of us, Drill Instructor," I shouted back. In hindsight, not the smartest thing I have ever said.

SSgt. went on a rampage. As I was standing at attention, he circled me, screamed at me, and insulted my whole family.

The incident of my wife's call came up, my defiance of the other drill instructors, and my absolute complete lack of military discipline came up from time to time. I stood there while he continued his rant for at least five minutes. It was the end of the day and you could tell he was tired of yelling. That's when he changed tactics. He visibly calmed down, backed away a little bit, and just softly spoke in a regular voice,

"Legge, do you know what we are trying to do here?"

They never called you just by your name. I knew this was a trick, but I was not going to back down.

I replied in just as calm a voice "I thought you were trying to make us Marines, Drill Instructor?"

One of the cardinal sins in boot camp is saying "I". You always had to start with the "The Candidate" did this or that. My using "I" was a complete slap in the drill instructors face. He knew it, I knew it, and worst of all, he knew that I knew. There wasn't even yelling that followed. He just looked at me and told me under no uncertain terms,

"You're outa here, Legge."

As I tell that story, some might think that I am proud of my defiance. In actuality, I am not. A real Marine has the inner strength to do what he is told, what is expected of him, and does not defy. He does his job.

CHAPTER THREE

MAY 2005
CHARLOTTE, NORTH CAROLINA

The unique part of a civil affairs group is the over abundance of officers in the unit. Out of roughly 190 Marines' total, around 63 were officers, most of who were used to being in charge of their reserve units back home. You couldn't swing a dead cat without hitting a Lt. Col. or above. This created an interesting environment, to say the least. One thing I will say for all those officers is that the next three months of training would turn a blind eye to rank and we would all come to treasure our upcoming training. We even had a t-shirt made after our training that said "6th CAG, 3 months of hell, 7 months in Iraq."

Our training was intense, comprehensive, exhausting and endless. We would do physical training in the early mornings, then go to class after class, then do more physical training in the late afternoon. Before I had left for Charlotte, I had taken what the Marine Corps calls MCMAP, which stands for Marine Corps Martial Arts Program, where I ended up breaking a couple of ribs, so throughout the training at Camp Lejeune, I could not take a deep breath without it hurting like hell. The physical portion of the training may have been hard but the indoctrination classes are what nearly killed us all. Marines don't mind bitching about running ten miles during the heat of day, but sit us down in a classroom for two hours where we are not allowed to destroy anything and you have a riot just waiting to happen.

We had language classes, cultural awareness classes, economic development classes, weapons classes, history classes, equipment classes, and more classes that I can't even remember. They would usually be followed by some sort of test to be certain that we had paid complete attention to all the subject matter. Like good Marines, we normally all passed the tests we were given. In fact, Marines are noted for our camaraderie and brotherhood, so it was not surprising to me at all when one entire row of Marines in one of the classes all got an 83 on their exam. Now that is sticking together.

Our training took us to not only other parts of the country, but some went as far as Finland for special training in the art of Civil Affairs. The most extensive training we went through, however, was in California where we went to SASO training. I hesitate to name the training that was done in the Mojave Desert in 100-plus degree weather, but since I don't know what it means, I don't think I am giving away any secrets. As a matter of fact, during the two-week training, I even asked one of the instructors what SASO stood for, and he did not even know. Marines love acronyms, but when it comes right down to it, I will bet my last dollar that half of them don't know what most stand for.

In a nutshell, the SASO training was conducted at an old military housing area from the fifties, which had been turned into a simulated Iraqi village. We would go through training exercises we were likely to encounter overseas. There were actual Iraqi citizens there who volunteered to help us understand the vastly different culture we were about to immerse ourselves in. We prepared ourselves for riots, respecting their mosques, women who would congregate and do their infamous "LAA-LAA-LAA-LAA-LAA" in front of imaginary camera crews, and even simple things like not taking food with your left hand so as not to offend anyone. There is no toilet paper in the Middle East, so the left hand is used for other things.

One exercise involved inviting the local Sheikhs to our CMOC (Civil Military Organization Command) for a friendly dinner to discuss the needs of the local Iraqis. We had been eating MREs (Meals Ready to Eat) for weeks and the thought of having a regular meal was something that I, in particular, was really looking forward to. I had been told that one of our Lance Corporals, LCpl Stout, had some cooking experience and he was going to prepare an appropriate meal. It was the best food I have ever tasted, just for the fact that it was not coming out of a brown bag. I begged for seconds once everyone else had been fed. I recall patting the LCpl on the back and telling him, "Stout, that was the best meal I have ever had, where did you get the food?" He simply replied, "Those where just MREs that I mixed together, sir." "No!" I quickly replied. "Say it ain't so, LCpl. Please say it ain't so." I literally begged Stout to tell me the meal I had just eaten had not been an MRE, but he refused to admit this was not true. I still think old Stout is a lying SOB.

The next day was probably the hardest day of my entire tour. It was around 113 degrees and we were doing convoy training, for which I was chosen as the convoy commander. One of our Lt. Col.'s who had no control over his emotions lost it and was yelling at me to move some vehicles about ten feet, but all the certified drivers were in another briefing. I sat there and took the berating from that Lt Col, listened to him go completely out of control, and then tried to explain to him that I had been briefed that only certified drivers were to even sit in the driver's seat of these humvees. This only made him go more ballistic, so I moved the humvees myself. After this exercise of futility, I was told that I needed to call home. An emergency had come up.

I called my oldest daughter and was informed that my second daughter, Amber, who was in New York at the Academy of Dramatic Arts, had just had a grand mal epileptic seizure and had been rushed to the emergency room. She was twenty years old and had never had any kind of seizure her whole life. I felt helpless, but training went on. That may sound heartless, but there is not a soldier who has ever gone to war and not had something happen at home, yet they do their duty. We had Marines who had their first children born while they were overseas. Others had loved ones suddenly die. Some got to fly home, but most simply went on doing their jobs. I think that is what I am most proud of when I look at the soldiers I was lucky enough to serve with. No matter what, they did their jobs.

CHAPTER FOUR

FEBRUARY 1984
QUANTICO, VIRGINIA

The weekend of our first liberty came and my life had been simply miserable. Most of which was my own doing. We began Saturday with high hopes that we would get liberty by noon. My wife was flying in that afternoon and was going to the hotel room. The inspection started out bad and continued to get worse. The only good part for me was that having a company billet, the company gunny would call me out of formation to run errands for him about every half hour. They were awful errands, but anything beats standing at attention for hours.

By five o'clock Saturday afternoon, it did not look like we were going to get liberty. We were right. We were again told that we were the worst outfit that ever went through Quantico and that if we did not get "unscrewed" by tomorrow, there would be no leave.

Sunday morning came, same routine, and I had just about had it. I think it is a little different for a married guy with children. I was beginning to think this whole deal was not worth it. I have a home and family to go back to. Things just seemed to get worse. By 11:00 in the morning, they were already telling us they were going to cancel all leave. I was in the commanding officer's office, being pushed around by both the gunny and Major Tracy himself, because they had knocked a hand full of chevrons (the emblems that go on our collars) out of my hands and onto the floor, and I was on my hands and knees trying to gather them up as they were making it impossible to hang on to them. Major Tracy was shouting at me that no one was going to get leave because I was so "screwed up" and it would take me all day to get "unscrewed." He was just trying to push me to see how much I could take. You would be

14

surprised how many grown men will break down and cry in situations like that. I would save my crying for 21 years later.

After about ten minutes of being shoved around, I shocked the hell out of Major Tracy. He was yelling at me for some reason, stating that none of us were going to get leave that day because of me when I said,

"The Candidate requests permission to make a phone call, sir."

Those steely grey eyes of his got as wide as I have ever seen a pair of eyes get. He could not believe what he was hearing. At first he did not know what to say, finally he just bellowed,

"What the hell are you talking about?"

"The Candidate requests permission to make a phone call to his wife so that she can go back home, sir!"

"What the hell are you talking about, Candidate?" He did not even know my name.

I explained, in proper format, that my wife had flown in from Oklahoma City the day before and was expecting me. I wanted to inform her I would not be there and to fly home.

This set Major Tracy off even more. He started yelling at me that it was entirely my fault that my wife was sitting in a hotel by herself and that if I was anything like a real Marine, I would be at the hotel right now and all the other Marines would be on leave as well.

By then I knew Major Tracy was just going through the motions of yelling at me. He had already yelled at the other three candidates that had company billets that week, telling them that it was all their fault that none of the Marines were on liberty. To this day, I think my stupid request to make a phone call got us at least an extra hour of leave that day. As soon as he stopped yelling at me about my wife, who had clearly married the wrong man, he instructed me to have all the platoons get in company formation.

I wish I could have recorded the speech Major Tracy gave that day when we finally got our first liberty. Before troops are let loose on liberty call, it is customary for the commanding officer to give a little pep talk/warning to the troops. Major Tracy had obviously done this before. He naturally went through all the safety warnings he was required to give. Don't drink and drive or you will get kicked out of the Marine Corps. Don't get into a bar fight or you will get kicked out of the Corps. Don't have fun or you will get kicked out of the Corps.

After a long list of what would get us kicked out of the Marine Corps, Major Tracy took great pleasure in warning us of the horrific problems that could arise from any dalliances we might consider with the opposite sex. He warned of the diseases, getting robbed, and worst of all, falling in love. After a full hour of warning us of what would ruin our leave, his final words were,

"Marines, you're going to find yourself in a bar. There are going to be all kinds of females there. You can spend all night going after the best looking woman in the bar and waste the majority of your leave, or you can abide by a long tradition that has kept this Corps intact, GUE. Go ugly early."

With that, he simply turned around and marched off. We were then sent to our own barracks where our drill instructors gave us their final briefing. It was short and sweet. Do anything that they ended up hearing about and we were dead. SSgt. Gerrards' final words were, "When you do come back from your little get away, we are going to ask you what you did. I expect to hear that you went to church, then to the library, and topped it off with going to Bingo! Dismissed."

All I can remember was that there were thirty Marines standing there, looking at each other and not having a clue what to do next. Were we really free to just leave? There had to be some kind of a catch to this. Freedom was something that had been beaten out of us weeks ago. I am not sure who made the first move, but when he did, we were like cockroaches when the lights come on.

I had borrowed a car that one of the other candidates had on base- Andy Hindman, whom I called Hinderman. Not sure why, but years later I saw him in California, and I kept calling him Hinderman. He thought I was an idiot. I headed for DC to see if my wife was still there. It was late Saturday afternoon, and we had to be back by 9:00 the next morning. I had around eighteen hours away from the Corps.

Well, my wife was at the hotel and quite frankly, I am not going to give you any details. I will say that I got a speeding ticket on the way back, because I used every minute I thought I could get away with out of those eighteen hours. I was certain that getting a speeding ticket would get me kicked out of the program and I literally begged the policeman not to give me a ticket. I not only got the ticket, but also had to put up with his immense pleasure in giving me the ticket. The last thing I said to him was that if he ever passed through Dallas, I sure hoped he would look me up.

I don't think I can really describe the mood I was in when I got back to the barracks. Everyone was dressed and ready for our 0900 muster, and they were waiting on me. They all started yelling that if I was not ready in ten minutes, we were all going to pay the price. I got dressed in slow motion. I was not in the mood to be rushed by anyone. I did get ready in time, however, and the welcome back to the Marine Corps formation began.

SSgt. Gerrard looked rejuvenated from his hours off as well. I am certain he had much less time than we had. We were all called to attention and the SSgt. went in front of Anderson and calmly asked, "Candidate, what did you do this weekend?" (Like it was a real weekend.). Candidate Anderson called out, "The Candidate went to church, the library and to Bingo, Platoon Sgt."

SSgt. Gerrard said nothing, turned to the next Candidate, positioned himself directly in front of him and asked the same question, "Candidate, what did you do this weekend?" The Candidate replied in the exact same fashion, "The Candidate went to church, to the library, and to Bingo, Platoon Sgt.!" This procedure went on for the next fifteen candidates, all with the same response. Then he came to me.

SSgt. Gerrard was aware of the fact that I had gone to DC to see my wife, so when he asked me, "Candidate, what did you do this weekend?" He had a wry smile on his face. "The Candidate fucked all weekend Platoon Sgt.!" were the words that came out of my mouth. A burst of laughter came from everyone in the barracks. I think even SSgt. Gerrard was caught off guard enough to let out a little laugh, because he had to go behind me, out of sight from everyone to regain his composure. Around fifteen seconds later, he came back around, stood in front of me, pressed his nose up against mine, and repeated the question, although this time he was anything but calm. "Candidate, what did you do this weekend?" he bellowed. The look in his eyes was absolutely unmistakable. If you don't answer the question the way I want you to then you are a dead man. Without hesitation, I yelled out even louder, "The Candidate fucked all weekend Platoon Sgt.!"

This time only a few laughed while the others were just planning on getting out the mops and buckets so that they could clean up my blood which was about to be spilled on the floor. SSgt. Gerrard did not even crack a smile. Sgt. Lynch, who was at the end of the formation, came running down to get in on the action. There was a little pause, and SSgt. Gerrard again got right in my face, gave me a long stare and yelled out again, "Candidate, WHAT… DID…YOU… DO… THIS… WEEKEND?" I could see in his eyes that he was done fooling around, but the words just came out again, "The Candidate fucked all weekend Platoon Sgt.!"

SSgt. Gerrard, if you are reading this book, I want to thank you personally for being such a professional Marine. I could tell that he wanted to take my challenge to the man-to-man level, in which case, he would have either killed me or at least kicked my butt like I had never had it kicked before. Sgt. Lynch was standing there as well, just ready to unload on me, but SSgt. Gerrard held him back, did not say a word, and just went to the next Candidate and asked the exact same question. The Candidate paused and said what he was suppose to say, "The Candidate went to church, the library, and then to Bingo, Drill Instructor!"

I spent the night cleaning out the latrine, and from time to time, Sgt. Lynch would pop in and let me know that there was no way that they were going to let me finish the program. He also said that I was lucky that SSgt. Gerrard had told him to keep his hands off of me, or they would have found my dead body in the dumpster the next morning.

The next day we had our usual PT (physical training) followed by a full Company run through the hills of Quantico. I was numb. I simply had enough, and I decided to teach all of them a lesson. When it came time to start the run, I intentionally got at the end of the line. With two hundred men running through the narrow paths that crisscrossed the hills of Quantico, the last man was at least four minutes behind the ponies they always put in the front. Hall, and I usually represented our platoon because we were the fastest. Hall was an unbeatable machine.

I decided that I would start dead last and sprint through the woods to see how many I could pass before my heart exploded. I was going to run until I dropped dead and that would teach the Drill Instructors. Imagine the paper work they would have to fill out.

I have never run so fast in my life. I was sprinting by one Marine after another. As planned, I was going to see how many I could pass before the inevitable. I ran and ran and ran. After three miles, there were only five Marines ahead of me. Two of who could run three miles in about fifteen minutes. Needless to say, I did not die in those hills of Quantico. Actually, just the opposite came true. I was reborn.

CHAPTER FIVE

Our primary mission in 6th CAG was to "win the hearts and minds of the Iraqi people." These words were repeated over and over again. We would do our best to heed them and not listen to those who preferred the slogan, "one in the heart, one in the mind." Our training was long and hard and after three months, we were all ready to get on a plane and do what we needed to do. We were to be sent to Al Anbar Province to go and win us some hearts and minds.

I remember, just before we left, talking to our commanding officer, Col. Brier about some economic development plans that I had once we got there. In my civilian career, I had come to know many corporate executives in a wide variety of fields and had already talked to several of them to see if they might be interested in being "sister companies" to some similar Iraqi companies that might need some assistance. For instance, a telecommunications company in the States might have equipment that would be considered outdated in America, but would be state of the art in Iraq. I was going into detail regarding the logistics of working the legal kinks out of a plan like this when Col. Brier stopped me and said, "I admire your enthusiasm, Legge, but I have been briefed to just try and not let Al Anbar Province fall into any more chaos than it already is."

I have to admit that this was a little unsettling. I may be naïve and way too optimistic, but I wanted to get something accomplished. I think we all felt that way. We believed in the mission and nothing was going to stop us from at least trying. I could tell Col. Brier really felt the same way.

We were all given the opportunity to go back home for one last chance to see our families before we boarded the plane that would cross the ocean we had been training next to. I could tell that my family, especially my older daughters, knew that I had already mentally left during the last few days when I was back in Dallas. I was focused and did not want to be distracted with anything.

We had a family get-together where I got to witness one of Amber's grand mal seizures. She fell to the ground, eyes rolled back, and all that I could do was hold her and keep her from swallowing her tongue. Most of my family lost it and went into panic mode. Not me. I just held my daughter on the floor, whispering to her that everything would be fine. I turned to my family members, ensuring them that everything would be fine. I meant it. I also believed it.

Amber did turn out to be fine, and it was time for me to go. I did not want any kind of send-off whatsoever. My two older daughters took me to the airport, and I headed back to North Carolina where we would finally begin our trip. I was not in uniform at the time so crying was not against the rules. I tried not to, but seeing my children crying was something that not even the strongest of Marines could have ignored. So much for the tough Marine image.

I went back to North Carolina where we spent hours and hours in lines collecting our weapons, ammo and gear, and we were ready to get on our way. We flew to a camp called Camp Victory in Kuwait where all soldiers pass through before they are sent to their final destination in the Middle East. It was an amazing sight to see just how many military personnel pass through Camp Victory. There were rows and rows and rows of temporary tents set up for those who were passing through. And the heat! I am not sure if those who are reading this know it or not, but the Middle East is kind of in the desert, and it gets hot there!

We spent a day or two in Kuwait until we finally had our aircraft ready to take us to our final destination. We were heading for Al Anbar Province, the wild west of Iraq. We loaded all our gear into a C-130, a workhorse aircraft that was working just as hard that day as it did in the Vietnam War some forty years earlier. There was one heck of a lot of gear. I was especially impressed with the fact that we all pitched in to get the aircraft loaded. I saw our commanding officer, a full bird colonel, grabbing the other end of a storage crate that was being lifted by a lance corporal. We were being sent to a place in which we were all going to rely on one another for our lives. Rank was not as important as survival.

6ᵗʰ CAG personnel in a packed C-130 on our way to Iraq.

Although I was in very good shape and felt as good as the teenagers I was going into battle with, I made the mistake of helping a two-hundred-twenty pound, nineteen year old, lean Marine, carry a medical supply crate to the awaiting aircraft. It was completely packed with medical supplies that were needed to last for the next eight months. Running to the aircraft was not so bad, other than the handle of the crate digging into my bare hands, but I could feel my shoulder tear as I lifted it up into the plane.

What a way to start my tour. I knew immediately that an old rotator cuff injury was going to plague me for months. After we had the helicopter fully loaded with supplies and Marines, the Commanding Officer, Col. Paul Brier, and I were the last to board the C-130 that was about to head into Iraqi airspace. Col. Brier was climbing up the ramp when he turned to me and said, "Legge, what time is it?" I quickly looked at my watch and responded, "0001 in the morning, sir," which meant that it had just passed midnight. "What day is it Legge?" asked the Col. without looking at me. I was not sure why he was asking me, and I had to look at my watch to see what day it was. "It is September 11th, sir." He looked at me, I looked at him, and not a word was said after that.

Now I have been on military flights before. Flying into a "hot zone" admittedly needs to be done as quickly as possible so that those on the ground don't get you locked into their sights, but this pilot took the "hot zone" landing to the extreme. He even gave us the defensive flares that are dropped in case we are being attacked by a heat-seeking missile. For all I know, someone did shoot a heat-seeking missile at us, but the way I was feeling at the time, I would have preferred for it to hit us. I am proud of the fact that I did not lose my lunch. However, I came close but managed to keep a little dignity going into a war zone not having to carry a barf bag with me.

One of our female majors was not so lucky with her first experience in putting her boots down on the war zone. Our C-130 was absolutely, completely packed with gear and personnel. We had to sit side by side, packed up against each, sitting on a long bench from one end of the aircraft to the other. In front of you was another bench from one end of the aircraft to the other. You actually had to place one knee in between the Marine's legs in front of you and the other knee in between the Marine next to him in order for all of us to fit into the plane. All our gear was in the center of the craft from the front to the rear and on the other side were two benches packed with Marines just as we were. Side by side, knees between the Marine's knees in front of you.

I don't think you could have fit a peanut butter sandwich in that C-130 after we were all aboard. It would not have been so bad, but we had some kind of mechanical problem that had to be attended to before we were cleared to take off. Now, I have been on commercial flights where we were delayed for one reason or another. It is irritating and to this day, I still don't like it and complain in my own seat with my headphones on, wondering why I have to be inconvenienced in this way. Then I think back to being stuck on that C-130, packed to the gill with sweaty, stinky Marines, about to go into an area where people shoot at you for no particular reason, and I always end up chuckling to myself.

This long wait was bad enough for most of us, but the female Major who had boarded the plane was told that this was only going to be a short thirty-minute hop. Believing this to be true because it came from one of her fellow soldiers in arms, she did not take the necessary precautions one might take preparing for a longer travel itinerary. I think you know where I am going with this. We sat for a couple of hours in that plane without so much as being able to move a muscle. We were finally given clearance to take off and make our short hop into Iraqi airspace. After landing at Al Assad airbase in Iraq, I exited the plane only to see the white backside of a fellow Marine, squatting on the runway, with the desert moon of Iraq acting as a black light. War is nothing like you would imagine it to be.

CHAPTER SIX

MARCH 1984
PENSACOLA, FLORIDA

Following graduation from OCS, where you are officially commissioned as an officer in the Marine Corps, you spend the next nine months of further training at The Basic School. No other branch of the military has such a school. The Marine Corps is designed so that every officer learns a little about each specialty in the Corps so that if a man goes down, another Marine can take his place. We spent those nine months learning everything from what a supply officer would do to an officer in charge of a sniper platoon. It was nine more months of physical training, classes, tests, and more classes.

Upon completion of The Basic School, we all finally headed to our designated MOS (Military Occupation Specialty) school. I was heading for Pensacola, Florida, where I was finally going to get to fly, or so I thought. Upon arrival in Pensacola, I learned that there was a yearlong wait to start the program. They even asked the Marines if they wanted to switch MOS's or join the Navy. A few did, but most of us would not budge. We were now Marines and that is what we would remain.

A typical day, those first few weeks in Pensacola, involved meeting at the football field at 0800 for morning muster, roll call was taken, and we were told to just stay out of trouble. The rest of the day was left with nothing to do. On occasion, some were called upon to put on their dress blues and help carry the coffin of a former Marine who was heading to guard the pearly gates.

Some enjoyed this easy life style. It drove me crazy. I begged for some kind of job but they had so many of us in Pensacola that they had simply run out of menial jobs to keep us busy. So I decided to head up to Milton, Florida, where we were sent once we completed ground school and actually got to fly.

It is a relatively small base with five fixed wing squadrons and two helicopter squadrons. I ran into Major Tripp at one of the squadrons and asked if there was anything he could have an energetic young second lieutenant do that would make his life easier.

For those of you who know anything about pilots, it is safe to say that what they like to do is fly. Paperwork is not one of their favorite past times. For those of you who know anything about the military, it is even safer to say that there is lots of paperwork. Lots and lots of paperwork. Major Tripp, who I had bumped into, happened to be the Senior Marine for VT-4. He was responsible for keeping all the ALMARs (all Marine memos) up to date, PFT's (physical fitness test) updated for all Marines in the squadron, and a host of other paperwork that was piled in a box on the floor by his desk.

The smile on his face when he said he thought he could find something for me to do came from the fact that he knew he now had a slave at his beck and call. I jumped into the job, organizing all the binders with current orders and regulations that had for years been neglected. I updated everything I could get my hands on. Soon word was out that Major Tripp had himself a slave. One by one, the Senior Marines from each squadron came to see if they could borrow the young 2nd Lieutenant to organize their paperwork.

I went from nothing to do to not having enough hours in the day to get everything done. I quickly submersed myself in project after project at the same time, getting to know how things worked at Milton. One thing I learned was how to get into a plane for my very first ride in a military aircraft. At the time, they were flying the T-34, a turbo propped aircraft that had been around forever. I think they are still using the same aircraft now that they were using twenty-five years ago in some places. When an aircraft had some kind of mechanical problem, they would take the craft to maintenance, see if they could fix it, then send someone up to see if the darn thing worked. This was my chance to finally get up in the air.

It was called a quality assurance flight. One of the instructors in Milton that wanted to get some extra flight hours would volunteer to take the plane up and do maneuvers to test the abilities of the plane. This involved maneuvers like stalls, loops and various other acrobatic maneuvers that you did not ordinarily do in flights at Milton. There was an empty back seat on these flights. I was going to get in that back seat and go for a spin.

A navy Lieutenant, our equivalent to a Captain, was about to take one of the planes up. I asked if he minded if I hopped along for a ride. He smiled at me, almost exactly like Major Tripp had done when I met him. You would think that I would have learned by then, but I wanted to get into the sky. He gave me the once over and I knew that he was going to mess with me, a tradition that had been carried down from generation to generation of pilots. I would play along, so long as I got up in those clouds.

First he sent me into the maintenance shop for the keys to the aircraft. There are times it is best to just go with the flow and not argue, so I went into the maintenance shop where several enlisted sailors were sitting around the coffee pot. "I need the keys to aircraft 219," I said, knowing there was no such thing as keys to an aircraft. The enlisted saw an opportunity to mess with a young officer and jumped at the chance. They were all looking everywhere for the keys to aircraft 219, going into the hangar, asking everyone if they had the keys to 219. Everyone delighted in sending me from one end of the hangar to the other, searching for those keys. After five minutes of screwing with the "butter bar," as they affectionately called us 2nd Lt's (because we had gold bars), they finally told me to tell the pilot just to hot wire the aircraft like he had done before.

I went back to the Lieutenant, who was doing a pre-flight check of the aircraft, and told him what they had said. He pretended to be annoyed that they had lost the keys once again. He then asked me if I had everything I needed for the flight. Helmet, check. Flight suit, check. Flight boots, check. Barf bag… I had not thought about that. He sent me back into the hangar to get a barf bag, just in case. Luckily, I grabbed two.

I climbed into the backseat of that T-34 and thought, at last, I have arrived. I hooked up the intercom system so that I could hear the instructions from the pilot. My job was to watch the gages and record things, such as the exact airspeed just as the aircraft stalled and began its reckless fall back to the earth. It rivals any ride you can find at any amusement park. There you are, flying along effortlessly through the air, the wind pushing the wings up to the heavens. As you power back the throttle, the craft goes slower and slower until the wind just does not have enough strength to keep the aircraft up, and after a slight shudder, the plane simply drops out of the sky and starts hurling itself towards the earth.

The other maneuvers we did were barrel rolls, the immelmann, dives and loops, until I was well on my way to using those barfs bags, which I was very glad I had. But the Lt. had a piece de resistance left in his repertoire. He took the aircraft to around 8,000 feet and took a steep dive. I was hoping he would not pull out of the dive and just crash into the earth, which seemed like it would make me feel better at the time. But, instead, at around 2,000 feet, he yanked back on the stick as hard as he could to give me my first real experience with the G-force.

For those who have never experienced around five G's, your body feels like it is five times heavier than it really is. Simple tasks like just raising your hand become a strain that is completely foreign to anything you have ever felt. All the blood drains from your brain and your vision begins to narrow down as if you are in a tunnel. I recall everything around me being completely black and my field of vision was now the size of a quarter.

After that, all I ever saw was the bottom of my barf bag. I do recall the Lt. calling me over the intercom to see if I was all right, and all that came out were guttural groans of a dying animal. I don't recall landing or taxing back to the hangar. I do recall the Lt. getting out of the plane and doing a post check of the aircraft, making certain he had not bent the wings with the G-force he had just put the plane through. This lasted around four or five minutes as my lifeless body remained in the backseat.

Eventually the Lt. climbed back up on the wing, slid the canopy back, banged his gloved hand on my helmet and shouted, "Get out of the aircraft, Lieutenant!" I have no idea how I managed to get out of the plane with my helmet still on and make my way back to my car, which was only around a hundred yards away. All I can recall was somehow getting the car door open and I collapsed inside. I glanced at the clock and it was three o'clock in the afternoon. The next conscious thought I had was seven o'clock that evening. I managed to get the car started and somehow it managed to find its way home, like a horse heading back to the barn.

I was either not strong enough to put the keys in the front door or I had left them in the car, but I had to ring the doorbell to my own front door. When my wife came to answer, she took one look at me and said, "Who shot you?" I was in no mood to talk so I stumbled back to the bedroom and passed out for another twelve hours.

Some are meant to fly, others are not. I went on several flights after that, both in fixed wing and helicopter, and although I never got as sick as that first flight and never had to use a barf bag until 22 years later, I never felt comfortable in the air. After thirty to forty minutes of pulling any G's, especially negative G's, a feeling would slowly begin to take over where my reflexes would slow down and my level of consciousness would diminish. I got used to it, but never conquered it.

At the same time, my wife became ill, partly from the stress of being a Marine wife, partly from simply missing what she considered to be our home. Regardless of the reasons, after only two years of active duty, and having to wait another year to start flight training, I opted to leave the Marine Corps. It was a very difficult decision to make, and an even harder decision to accept as the years would roll by.

CHAPTER SEVEN

SEPTEMBER 2005
RAMADI, IRAQ

Our stay at Al Asad was short. We unloaded our C-130 with all our gear and sat in staging areas. Before each of the smaller units departed, we were placed in a large dome-shaped barracks (much like what Gomer Pyle lived in) where I sat on a cot reading "The Kite Runner," a book that my daughter Amber had given me. About two hundred yards away from our hut, two explosions went off almost simultaneously. It was those whom we were about to meet saying, "Hey."

Me an hour after arriving in Iraq after our first mortar rounds.

My trip was to take me to the city of Ramadi, just ninety miles west of Baghdad. A few hours later, we loaded our CH-46 helicopter with all our gear, and we were off. This sounds a little easier than it really was. One thing that those who have never been deployed to Iraq will ever completely understand is how difficult it is to get from point A to point B. The ninety miles from Baghdad to Ramadi is just a quick car ride for those of us used to freedom. In Iraq, every movement, regardless of how near or far, was a labor of frustration. Our helicopter ride, for instance, took place at 0300. That is three o'clock in the morning for you civilians.

We arrived at Camp Blue Diamond, a base along the Euphrates River in the city of Ramadi, one of the largest cities in Iraq with over 400,000 people, at around 0330. Although it was a large city, it was on the border of the vast desert that expanded west all the way to the Syrian border. The darkness of the desert is a sight to see, or more accurately, a sight not to see. I think we are just used to the residual lights of all the street, town and house lights here in America. In Iraq, the electricity was out well over half the time, so at night, it was completely dark. For security reasons, we also were limited in the use of flashlights. So, my first experience of Ramadi was in total darkness.

View of Camp Blue Diamond from the archway at north end of base.

The trip from the helicopter pad to our living quarters was only three fourths of a mile, but we had to carry all the gear we had brought for the next eight months. I cannot carry even one of my daughter's suitcases which she needs for a weekend getaway; imagine carrying everything you will need for eight months. Some of the older Marines (there were a few my age) had a real problem making the trip. Since they were generally of a much higher rank, we had to listen to their griping and the younger Marines helped with their gear. In the total darkness, and despite the agony of carrying way too much gear, my eyes began to get used to the stark darkness and shadows of the landscape began to appear.

You could see the outlines of tall palm trees that lined the narrow road running from one end of the base to the other. You could also see grand structures with elaborate masonry work against the background of the desert. I was uncertain what I was to expect when reaching my final destination after all our hard training, but I certainly never expected thinking that it would be beautiful. We finally reached our trailers and were given our assigned living quarters. It had been a long hard two days of travel with very little sleep and the fact that I now actually had a bed that I could call my own should have made me crawl in and sleep, but I was too geared up about my new surroundings. I decided to keep my battle gear on and do some exploring.

Ramadi was one of the primary residential locations where Saddam Hussein and his sons spent most of their leisure time, if you could call it that. His residence, converted to Camp Blue Diamond, was close to a mile long peninsula that had the fast-flowing Euphrates river running on the east side and a tributaries of the Euphrates that we simply called The Canal along the west side. There were two main residential palaces where Saddam and his sons lived and a score of other residential buildings for servants and "guests." I was eventually told by some of the local residents, with whom I became friends, that several of the buildings were used to house women for entertainment for the two sons. I was told it was very common for a woman to be taken off the street, placed in one of these housing units, and would never be heard from again. As I said earlier, the Euphrates was an incredibly fast-flowing river.

But that night I knew nothing of the history of this place. As I walked around the secured walls of this base, the sun working its way to morning slowly broke the darkness. I could see the remnants of the major palace that had received a direct hit from one of our JDAM bombs which had taken out part of the roof of the palace (as they are designed to do), only to work its way to the lower floors where it unleashed most of its force. But the palace itself remained 90 percent intact. It was quite a beautiful sight. I had been to the Middle East before but had not seen the traditional Babylonian-style architecture of what had been called the Cradle of Civilization. I was impressed.

J-DAM Palace" This was one of the residential
palaces of Saddam Hussein and his sons.

As I walked around Camp Blue Diamond, in awe of its beauty and feeling
the thousands and thousands of years of history that blanketed this oasis in
the desert, I completely lost sight of why we were there. I pictured a time
when there was tremendous pride in this place because of their intellectual
and educational accomplishments in the world they lived. It seemed a shame
we had to put such large holes in its roofs. As the sun started to come up, the
peacefulness of the night was ran off by more and more Marines filling the
narrow street of the base. All in heavy combat gear to protect them from the
occasional 60m mortar or rocket-propelled grenade that would be lobbed in
over the vast walls that surrounded the base.

I was quickly brought back to the present. We spent a couple of days at
Camp Blue Diamond, organizing our trip that was going to take us only three
miles to the east where the Government Center was located in the streets of
downtown Ramadi. I was enjoying the stay at Camp Blue Diamond because
it had nice housing, great food and a place where you could check out movies,
play ping-pong, and it even had a pool table known as MWR. I was told
not to get used to it because where we were heading, things were a little less
convenient.

At the time we were in Iraq there were on average around seventy-five significant events a day. A significant event was any time a coalition forces soldier was either shot at with an AK-47, hit by an IED (Improvised Explosive Devise), had a rocket propelled grenade launched at them, or had a suicide car bomb hurled at him. Anything that could kill you was casually referred to as a "significant event." Over the next eight months I was to come to the realization that out of those seventy-five recorded significant events in Iraq, our little building would average around twelve to fifteen. Every single day.

The preparation for our convoy to the Government Center seemed a little over the top. The unit that was leading the convoy for several hours briefed us. We were told what to watch out for, plans if we were to get hit, alternate plans if this happened and even alternate plans in case the alternate plans failed. We would start rolling at exactly 0300. That meant we would need to assemble at least 45 minutes prior to departure. That would turn out not to be much of a problem because the adrenaline was already starting to pump through our veins.

We all gathered at the designated staging area with plenty of time to spare. All our gear was checked and rechecked. All communication equipment was checked and rechecked. We were told to get into our designated vehicles. Mine was what is called a "seven-ton." It is a large truck that is primarily used for transporting troops. It is one of the safest vehicles because it has a lot of armor to protect the troops. The only problem with all the armor is that it makes visibility for the troops in the back almost nonexistent. This meant that our trip to the Government Center might be safer, but as far as scenery, all one could expect to see was the boots of the Marine in front of you. This did not seem to be a concern at the time but I would come to regret it a week later.

CHAPTER EIGHT

SEPTEMBER 2001
BEDFORD, TEXAS

Fifteen years passed by after I left Pensacola. I was in the Individual Ready Reserves for six years after I left active duty, where all you do is show up once a year to muster filling out paperwork all day, then go back to being a civilian. I had four kids. Not part of this story. Started a national property tax consulting firm. Not part of this story. Was on the cover of several magazines. Not only not part of this story, but also not true. Then came 9/11. It is a shame that what is a great Porsche will now always be three numbers that we will remember as being the beginning of the unknown. I was laying in my bed with my one-year-old son, reading him a book, when my secretary called and told me to turn on the television. Her husband works for United Airlines and he heard right away about the plane crashing into the World Trade Center. I turned on the TV, watched with interest, and then watched in horror as the second plane hit the other tower.

At that very moment I knew that the world was going to be different for my son and three daughters. They were not going to live under the same circumstances as I did. My thoughts then turned to my cousins who not only worked in Manhattan, but were very close to the World Trade Center. Both got off at the subway at the World Trade Center, and then walked to their offices. One had not yet left that fateful morning, the other was not heard from for at least eight hours, as she had to walk out of the city.

Clients that I had worked with, most of whom I only knew through our phone conversations, were on the floor of the tower the plane had chosen to hit. Several weeks later I was asked to provide financial information as to what assets they had at that facility because all other records were lost. These incidents do not compare to the thousands and thousands of others that actually lost love ones on that day.

I was very proud of our President for not making a hasty decision on what type of retaliation was required at that stage in history. I met his father, also a former President of the United States, at a golf tournament in Houston. The Naval Academy was having a fund raising tournament and the former President came to show his support. I was invited because my best friend happened to be the tight end for two Heisman Trophy winners, Joe Bolino and Roger Staubach, at the Naval Academy. Gary Kellner is a retired Commander, fighter pilot, and not that bad of a golfer. Gary caught two touchdown passes; on both offense and defense (back when they played both sides of the ball) the last time Navy beat Notre Dame back in 1963. At least that was true until 2004 when Navy actually ended the longest losing streak between two college teams.

I didn't have much of a chance to talk to the former President until he was leaving the crowd of people that had coerced him into dozens and dozens of pictures. The secret service did their usual diplomatic job of getting the crowd to give the President a break. I was standing off to the side against the wall to make room for the President and his entourage when the President saw that I had a Marine Corps golf shirt on, and stepped over towards me and asked if I was a Marine. I told him that I had served under him, and if I had it my way, would also serve under his son. He took my hand, shook it and said, "Well God bless you son. Once a Marine, always a Marine." By then the secret service had him by the arm and was dragging him to the waiting limo. What the President had said, "Once a Marine, always a Marine," is something that burns deep down inside every Marine, regardless of age, especially when he knows his fellow Marines are off to war.

I have shaken hands with all sorts of people in my life. Some famous, some not. Some rich, some so desperately poor that you wonder how they could possibly survive. When I shook President George Bush Seniors' hand, it meant more to me than any other hand I had ever shaken. The reason is because just thirty minutes prior to shaking his hand, the President had given a very impromptu speech to those at the dinner that had attended the golf tournament. He spoke of his pride in those who served their nation. He said that of all the things he had done as the President of the United States, sending troops into Iraq in 1991 for Desert Storm was by far the most difficult decision he had ever made in his lifetime. As he talked about the 143 soldiers that had given their lives in the operation, tears filled the Presidents eyes. His voice began to tremble, and he looked out into the audience of primarily military men and just said, "Thank you."

Not to take anything away from those 143 brave men and women, and especially not to make light of the family members of those 143, but 143 is not a large number. In terms of warfare, the President should have talked proudly of the fact that only 143 were killed. Shouldn't he? I only shook the man's hands for a moment, and only heard some off-the-record remarks he made at a golf tournament, but I would venture to say that if only one soldier died during Desert Storm, President George Bush Sr would have still shed that tear. He would still put that one soldier's life and family left behind in his prayers for the rest of his life.

It was this type of patriotism that made me come up with the crazy idea of getting back into the Corps. I knew that it would not be easy; I knew that it was completely insane for a 45-year-old to put on a uniform again after nearly twenty years had passed, and I knew that I was going to receive a lot of resistance. I did not know just how much resistance I would have and from how many sides it would come.

Several months after 9/11, I took a casual drive to the Fort Worth Joint Reserve Base, formerly Carswell Air Force Base, and strolled into the Marine Corps prior service recruiters' office. There was a Lt. Col. in the office who was obviously in charge, but it appeared that the rest of his staff were out doing PT. He saw me wandering around the hallways and asked if there was anything he could do for me. I stepped into his office and after a bit of small talk, him asking me what I currently did, me telling him I was the CEO of a small consulting firm, the only thing I could think to say at the time was, "Do you need any old Marines that still have a little life left in them?"

I once went up to a super model at a convention and asked if she would care to go out for dinner. I am almost certain that the Lt. Col. made the exact same expression she had given me when I asked him that question. Seeing the look on my face, and that I was serious, he quickly regained his composure and asked, "Exactly how old are you?" I replied that I was forty-five, but still in good shape. If I could not get my three-mile run time under twenty-one minutes, I would not even consider getting my commission back. If I was going to go back into the Corps as a Lieutenant, I was going to be in as good a shape as a real Lieutenant, even if I was twenty years their senior.

The problem with being an officer, rather than enlisted, is that after a certain period of time, you lose your commissioning as an officer if you do not put in a certain amount of active or "good" time. I had lost my commission many years ago and in order for me to be brought back into the Marine Corps, I would have to be recommissioned. At my age, this would either take an act of Congress, or an act of God.

The Lt. Col. quickly said that he appreciated me coming in, but that there was no way I would ever be brought back in. I was a little embarrassed but appreciated his honesty. I then said that if there was anything I could do behind the scenes, I would be glad to help. He said that the only thing he could think of was the Marine Corps Toys for Tots campaign they had every year. He said they could always use extra help for that. He told me to come back in a couple of months and he would steer me to the proper people.

I left his office and mumbled to myself all the way to the car. "You stupid idiot. As you get older, you are supposed to get wiser you dumb son of a bitch." What on earth was I thinking? I drove back to my comfortable home, and for a while, put the crazy idea of becoming a Marine again out of my mind. I was a civilian and that is what I was going to remain.

A few months went by and Christmas was getting closer and closer. The end of the year is not a busy time for me, and I thought about what the Lt. Col. had said about needing volunteers for the Toys for Tots campaign. It is an incredibly good cause, and I thought it would be good for my kids to get involved as well. I drove to the base and went back to the Lt. Col.'s office. He, however, was not there. Lt. Col. Belinda Ingalls had replaced him. Lt. Col. Ingalls is a no-nonsense, get-things-done kind of Marine. She asked what she could do for me, I told her that I had met with a Lt. Col. a couple months ago and that he had asked for me to come back and see him. She asked my rank, age and MOS. I quickly said, "No, Ma'am, you don't understand. I just thought I could volunteer to help with the Toys for Tots campaign." She said, "So you are not interested in getting back into the Corps?" She caught me by surprise. I was not sure what to say so I said, "I would be glad to serve again if you think the Corps could use me."

Lt. Col. Ingalls told me that the Corps was desperate for reserve officers 01, 02, and 03. That is 2nd Lt., 1st Lt. and Captain. She said there were hundreds of billets currently not being filled because of the lack of junior grade officers. I said that it would be hard to pass me for a "junior" but if the Corps could actually use me, I would be glad to give it a try. She explained that there were several outfits in her territory that were in desperate need of me. My heart started pounding. She said that the first thing I had to do was interview with the senior officer at a unit that needed a junior grade officer, and if he or she liked me and would write a letter of endorsement, they would put together a package and send it to headquarters.

By then my head was spinning. This was not just some crazy idea or bar room talk. This was for real. Lt. Col. Ingalls said she would make some calls and see what units were in the most need, and that she would get back with me. I walked out of that office to my car, much as I had some twenty or so years ago after my first flight, in a complete daze. This was a big, big decision. Not so much for me, but for my family and business that I had spent the past twenty years growing and nurturing. I was not sure who would be most against this insanity- my business associates or my family.

I had been a single parent for a long, long time after my wife and I had divorced. I was a very big part of all my children's lives and their well-being was the most important thing to me. I knew that if I was brought back into the Corps, the chance that I might have to leave them for a year for an overseas tour was more than just a remote possibility. As for my business, I knew that I was semi-important to my company, but I had a great group of employees and a great partner who were more than just co-workers; they were like family. Besides, how much does the boss really do anyway?

It was my children I worried about the most. I had two older daughters, Tiffany age 23 who was about to graduate from Texas A&M, and Amber age 20, who was heading off to New York to the acclaimed Academy of Dramatic Arts to study acting. Tiffany was the level-headed one, and Amber was going to end up either on Broadway receiving a Tony or at the Academy Awards, accepting an Oscar. My only concern with Amber was that she might win the award while I was overseas, and I would not get to attend. I know every parent says that about their kids, but no kidding, she is that good of an actress.

Tiffany is my responsible child. I have had to encourage her over the years to be a little more like Dad and screw up every now and then. She tried, but she is like a rock. Through a set of completely unrelated circumstances, which would take another entire book to write, I also had two more children. Easton, my third daughter, was 11, and my son Joshua was just turning two. Easton lived primarily with her mother, unlike Tiffany and Amber in their growing years. She is the smartest of all my kids. I can say that without hurting any of my other kids' feelings because they see it as well. She was far older than her years would let you believe, but she was about to go through those horrible teenage years.

Joshua, however, was just so young. He spent quite a bit of time with me because one of the incredible advantages of being the boss is that you can set your schedule around things. I worked at home a lot because the office was only three miles away. If something came up that required me in the office, I would just pack him up and take him with me. All the women in the office loved having him around, more than having me around. Joshua's mother is a choir director and very busy during the day, so things worked out perfect. But what if I were gone?

I drove home and knew that I had to talk to my kids about what I was preparing to do. I talked with Tiffany and Amber first. They were surprisingly supportive about getting back into the Corps. They were proud of me for wanting to do my part. Easton really did not know what to think about it but supported me as well. Joshua had just learned to talk and had other things on his mind. With the support of my direct family, I saw no reason to discuss it with too many people in case this turned out to be a wild goose chase, which was a distinct possibility.

CHAPTER NINE

SEPTEMBER 2005
THE GOVERNMENT CENTER, RAMADI, IRAQ

The convoy from Camp Blue Diamond to the Government Center, although exciting, was completely uneventful. From the time we pulled out of the south gate of Blue Diamond till we entered the well-guarded gate of the Government Center, only around five minutes had passed. The most thrilling part of the trip was the sounds of the roaring engines from all the vehicles racing down what you could tell were city streets. The only thing you could see from the seven ton were the tops of two-story buildings. There were bullet holes in every building I could see. Some of the buildings had obviously been hit by air strikes. Tops of some of the buildings were completely missing. We were in a bad neighborhood.

After our vehicles were in the courtyard of the Government Center, the makeshift but extremely heavy gate was rolled back into place. There was barbed wire everywhere. We were told to quickly jump out of our vehicles and head to the front door of the Government Center. It was still dark but you could tell that this was not going to look like the State Capital in D.C.. And the smell was overwhelming. We would later find out the splashes we heard under the tires of the vehicle as we approached the Government Center was not water. The sewage ran down the center of the street directly in front of the building that was now my new home. We were moving into a sewer!

We quickly shuffled into the dark building that smelled slightly better than the street outside. This was the Capital Building of one of the largest provinces in all of Iraq. We made our way down the hallways that were lined with cots. Although you could not see very well, you could see that each cot, lined up head-to-toe all the way down the hall on both sides, were filled with sleeping Marines. This did not look like a four star hotel. I was expecting someone to steer me to an empty cot, when we were suddenly outside again in a smaller courtyard. We were heading to a smaller building that was lit by the noisy and smelly diesel generator growling in the courtyard.

We entered what was to be our home for the next eight months. It was not the Taj Mahal but it did not look too bad. It was known as the PCMOC (Provincial Civil Military Operation Center). A couple of Marines we were to relieve were barely awake but led us to the quarters we would occupy. Eight of us were directed to a room that was 12 feet by 20 feet, which is roughly the size of a decent walk-in closet. Two sets of two bunk beds lined each wall with just enough room in the middle for two people to stand. This was alright if you were standing but getting dressed in the morning was like doing a slow dance with a partner you really did not want to look at.

My home at the Government Center, along with seven other Marines.

I took the top bunk in the corner by a boarded-up window that had been sprayed with foam sealant that was dripping down the wall. It looked like a mess and I wondered why they had sprayed all that foam around the plywood boarding the window. Later that night I found out what the foam was for. We were given a Welcome to Ramadi party by those who wanted it to be our farewell party. We were hit with rocket-propelled grenades, AK-47s, IEDs, and everything they had on hand. The attack lasted for hours. The foam did a pretty good job of keeping the dust from flying all over my bed but it taught me that if I did not want my head covered with dust and dirt at night, it would be best to sleep with my feet closest to the window.

The small arms fire was really not that bad. You could hear the rounds hitting the walls, but we were very well protected from such attacks. What really made things rumble and throw up dust were the IEDs. Because our building was on Route Michigan, which had more IED explosions than any road in Iraq, these explosions became routine. That first night, they knew a new unit had moved in and they wanted to scare us off. The results were just the opposite.

Because we had to be up at 0700 the next morning, I only got three hours of sleep that night. I slept like a baby, in spite of the attack going on outside. As a member of a CAG unit, we were not allowed to engage with the enemy unless all hell had broken loose. I had already met the Marines of 3/7 who were assigned to protect us while we had been in training in California. I met one of the commanders of the unit, Capt. Ash, a hard core Mustang Marine who had come up through the enlisted ranks and knew what he was doing. I slept like a baby the entire time I was at the Government Center. Thank you, 3/7 Marines, for all the sleep.

That morning we got to see what this Government Center actually looked like. Our building was a square building with small rooms around the exterior, and a conference room and lobby in the center. It was roughly the size of an average-sized restaurant. It also had a small kitchen with two refrigerators. There was a courtyard between our building and the Government Center. We were instructed that we had to be in full combat gear in order to cross the very short distance and we were recommended to run. Seeing the thousands of bullet holes in the walls of the courtyard was all we needed as proof that this would be a good idea.

Our kitchen at the Government Center with LCpl
Thrift enjoying one of our fantastic meals.

Once you crossed the courtyard, you entered the Government Center. It was a two-story building that was covered with dirt, inside and out. It was partially used for the 50 or so 3/7 Marines who rotated in and out of the Government Center. I believe they would rotate in 50 Marines every four days. The conditions those poor Marines had to endure was unbelievable. The remaining three-fourths of the building was for the Iraqi government officials of Al Anbar Province. It also held the office of the Governor of Al Anbar Province, Gov. Rashid Ma'Moun. It would turn out that Governor Ma'Moun and I would become good friends.

Governor Ma'Moun and I shaking hands at the end of my tour.

Although the Government Center appeared to be filthy, so was the PCMOC that housed only Marines. Marines are noted for their shiny boots, pressed uniforms and squared-away quarters. How is it that our quarters always looked so dirty? It was not for lack of effort. Every morning before we started "conducting business," every single Marine stationed at the PCMOC had cleaning detail. We were all assigned our area and cleaning utensil, and we cleaned. Our Commanding Officer, Col. Miles Burdine, was given a broom every morning and his job was to sweep the kitchen.

Bronze Star

Burdine honored for service in Iraq

■ "It wasn't just me. I was simply part of an organization, the 6th Civil Affairs Group."
— Col. Miles Burdine

By RICK WAGNER
rwagner@timesnews.net

KINGSPORT — Marine Col. Miles Burdine received the Bronze Star Friday for his service in Iraq.

He worked with the Al Anbar provincial government, living in the province capital of Ramadi, which he said was roughly the U.S. equivalent of helping Tennessee state government and living in Nashville.

But Burdine, in civilian life the executive vice president and chief executive officer of the Kingsport Area Chamber of Commerce, took the opportunity of the ceremony to promote the planned Kingsport Veterans Park and Memorial in J. Fred Johnson Park near Dobyns-Bennett High School.

Groundbreaking is set for the spring of 2007, with completion to come in 2008. It will honor the 347

Please see BURDINE, page 2A

Marine Col. Miles Burdine, with members of his family in attendance, receives the Bronze Star Friday for 'meritorious achievement' in Iraq's Al Anbar province from August 2005 to February 2006.

Colonel Burdine receives the Bronze Star for his
achievements in Al Anbar Province.

I became known as "Dust Pan Man." My job was to take a dust pan and paint brush, and sweep up all the piles of dust that those who were assigned a broom and a room had swept into a nice, neat pile. Not to brag or anything, but my responsibilities were the only duties that covered the entire building. Anyone can take care of a single room, but a whole building takes not only precision but also speed. For my fellow Marines who were stationed with me and are reading this book, sorry for telling it like it is, but you know it is the truth.

Because my duties as Dust Pan Man were spread over the entire building, it was important to get the dust pile quickly or Marines would trample through the pile and spread it all over the building. I would sprint from room to room, drop down on my knees in front of my pile and sweep up the dust, dash to the nearest trash bag, dump the dust, and head to the next pile requiring my expertise. As I dashed through the PCMOC, I would call out "Here comes Dust Pan Man…. Dust Pan Man." It did not take long for the Marines who had the brooms, especially the higher ranking sweepers, to get a kick out of calling for Dust Pan Man. Someone came up with a cackling call that sounded like a large bird dying and that was my signal that Dust Pan Man was needed. I would dash to the sound of the call, singing, "Dust Pan Man… Dust Pan Man!"

Dust Pan Man

The problem over there is that as soon as you clean up completely, ten minutes later you can write your name on whatever you just cleaned because of the dust. It was like moon dust and it got everywhere. So for those who say that Middle-Easterners are dirty in some way or another, you try and stay clean over there.

CHAPTER TEN

MARCH 2002
COLORADO SPRINGS, COLORADO

Did I mention that there is quite a bit of paperwork in the military? If you are not part of the government, you can't even begin to fathom how much paperwork a government agency can create. But before the paperwork, I had to interview with a unit that not only needed a Lt., but also did not mind that he was 45 years old. LtCol Ingalls said that a unit in Colorado Springs had been begging for a junior grade officer for nearly two years, so I was off to Colorado Springs.

Colorado Springs was a little farther from Dallas than I would have liked. If I did get into this unit, I would have to be there once a month and two weeks in the summer, which was fine by me. I was starting to believe this was really going to happen.

Upon arrival at the unit in Colorado Springs, I was greeted with what is best described as curiosity. I felt like a panda bear in front of someone who had never actually seen one. I was escorted to a conference room where I was introduced to the Commanding Officer of the unit, the XO, and at least three others who wanted to see the panda bear. I was asked question after question.

"What is your MOS?"

"7599" (meaning student naval aviator, which to this day is still my primary MOS).

"Are you really 42?"

"Yes."

"What is your current civilian job?"

"I am the President/CEO of a property tax consulting firm headquartered in Dallas."

This answer got them talking amongst themselves.

"How long has your company been in business?"

"Almost twenty years now."

The next several questions centered on my company, what companies I had represented, yada, yada, yada. Then came the question that they just had to ask, as many have asked me to this date, "Why on earth do you want to get back into the Marine Corps?"

All I could say was, "Once a Marine, always a Marine."

The rest of the interview was spent grilling me on things, like would I be able to make it to their monthly drills? I assured them that I would. Would I go to specialized training on the East Coast? I said I would. Question after question, and I did the best I could to answer them as openly and honestly as possible.

The last question they asked me were, "Do you realize that there is a good chance they would send you to Iraq? Would you be willing to go?"

"Yes, sir."

The interview was over. I really had no feel for how it went. I am usually very good about evaluating how meetings go, but that's with civilians. I was among Marines again. Never try and figure out what a senior Marine is thinking, if he wants you to know, he will tell you.

When I arrived back in Dallas, LtCol Ingalls instructed me to brief her on how the interview went. I could only report that I had no clue whether they wanted to kill me or hire me. Two weeks later, a very strong endorsement to have me brought back into the Marine Corps came in the mail. My package was about to begin.

I had to go through physicals, create resumes (something I had not done in twenty years), fill out what seemed like hundreds of questionnaires, have pictures taken, and basically explain what I had in my underwear drawer. LtCol Ingalls had even more paperwork to do. Waiver forms (due to my age), time out of service and lack of a usable MOS had to be prepared. I think the fact that she was new to this position was the only reason things had progressed as far as they had. After what seemed like forever, my package was ready to be sent.

There was no fanfare, just a bunch of papers stuffed in an envelope, but to me this was a life-altering moment. For the past 15 years, after being expunged from the Marine Corps, I had a deep-seated feeling of having abandoned the Corps. I had quit. I had left the Marines, with whom I had gone through Officer Candidate School, The Basic School, and part of Flight School, behind to carry the burden of defending our country. I could easily rationalize this decision by saying there were no extended wars that had been fought, with the exception of Grenada and the Gulf War, in the time that I was out. But that would demean the efforts that our military stands for in keeping the peace that we all enjoy every single day. I still felt that I had an obligation, for whatever reason or for whatever cause, to do what the Marine Corps expected of a Marine.

This guilt complex led to a more real and present problem. Was I prepared and capable of performing the duties that I would have to do? This was by far the biggest obstacle I personally had to overcome. The fact that I owed the Marine Corps something meant absolutely nothing to anyone but me. The question was- did I truly have something to offer that would benefit the Corps?

One of the first indoctrinations of a Marine is that every Marine is a rifleman. That means that we are all trained to be at the lowest level of warfare, the one who has to pull the trigger and kill the enemy. This seems like a basic responsibility of a soldier, but the responsibilities that go with such a simple concept are far more complex than one might imagine. It involves working as a team, and most importantly, protecting your fellow Marines. The saying that you are only as strong as your weakest link means something different to a soldier. I did not want to be the weakest link.

Over the next several weeks, as I waited for the response from Quantico, the headquarters of the Marine Corps, I began to work on getting back in shape. If, as you read this, you hear the theme song to "Rocky" in the background, I can assure you it is not "Rocky I." "Rocky XI" would be more appropriate. But, at the age of 42, I was still in pretty good shape. I could run three miles at an 8 minute pace, but I was determined to bring it down to twenty one minutes total, which was a seven minute pace. In my younger years, I could get a perfect score of three hundred on the PFT, which required 20 pull-ups 80 sit-ups in two minutes, and running three miles in under eighteen minutes.

The pull-ups had become a problem because of a shoulder injury, but the sit-ups were not a problem. As for ever running three miles in under eighteen minutes, I had given up on that idea long ago. After a couple of weeks of working out regularly again, I felt that I was ready to keep up with the young lieutenants whom I would now be competing with, and more importantly, would not be a poor example for the young enlisted who are the center of the Corps. All that was left was for Headquarters to give the green light, and I was ready.

After three weeks, I finally received a call from LtCol Ingalls. My package had been denied. It was a short and sweet letter. Thanks, but no thanks. I have to admit, I really did have my hopes up and really did expect to be commissioned again. From what LtCol Ingalls had said about how desperate the Corps was for reserve officers and what I had seen going to a unit that had been trying to fill a slot for nearly two years, I thought I would wear the uniform again.

LtCol Ingalls was pissed. She could not understand how, on the one hand, she and all other prior service recruiters were being criticized for not meeting their quotas on junior grade officers, and then being denied what she considered to be a viable applicant. I, on the other hand, felt like shit. I have failed at certain things in my lifetime, but never at something that really mattered to me. This mattered. LtCol Ingalls, a stubborn perfectionist, was not willing to accept this decision. She immediately said that we had to submit another package, only this time the package was going to be immaculate. She had now been in the prior service recruiting business a little longer and knew what had to be done. I, on the other hand, really did not want to be turned down again. Lt. Col. Ingalls assured me she knew what she was doing and this time, they could not turn us down.

My age seemed to be the main problem. So to prove to headquarters I was still in shape, we came up with the idea of me doing a regular Marine Corps PFT and submitting my score with the next package. The only problem was, due to legal reasons, I could not actually take the PFT with the Marine Unit at the Fort Worth Joint Reserve base. If I was to have a heart attack and die on the run (something I had failed at twenty years prior), the Marine Corps could not accept the responsibility. I had to administer the test on myself, and we would simply submit it as a "simulated PFT result." I was to do as many pull-ups as possible, then do as many sit-ups as I could in two minutes, then time my three-mile run.

We also decided that I would interview with yet another unit, one that was in even more dire need of an officer. It was a unit in Wichita, Kansas. It was around an eight-hour drive to the unit, and I thought if I was going to go there once a month, at minimum I needed to get used to the drive. I had an interview with a Mustang Marine Capt (again, a prior enlisted Marine who became an officer) who was what we Marines call "good to go." When I arrived for the interview, he immediately told me he would endorse me just for the fact that I made the drive. He said that many of the Marines in the unit found some kind of an excuse not to show up for drills. I assured him that that would not be the case with me. We talked for a couple of hours about what my responsibilities would be and I learned a lot about this Capt. He was a down-to-earth Marine who had dedicated his life to the Corps. I really wanted to work with this Marine.

CHAPTER ELEVEN

SEPTEMBER 2005
THE GOVERNMENT CENTER, RAMADI, IRAQ

The Government Center was where the "elected" officials of the Iraqi Government for Al Anbar Province conducted their business. Al Anbar Province was primarily made up of what are called Sunni Muslims. They only represent around 20 percent of the people in Iraq but they were at least 90 percent of the population of this province. Saddam Hussein and his sons were Sunni. The rest of the population in Iraq is Shiites and Kurds. I could go into detail as to the difference between Shiites, Sunnis, and Kurds, when there was a split and why, but to tell you the truth, I think that just simplifies things and gives us a catch word for a quick news bite.

In virtually all news reports I saw back home it was "Shiites did this" or "Sunnis did that." Many times, they were wrong about which group bombed this mosque or the suicide bomber at this location belonged to that group. It is so much like our Republican versus Democrat argument in the States. Quite frankly, it is just not worth my time trying to explain one group's ideology versus another, especially when we are supposed to be the land of the free.

The elected officials at the Government Center were given the title of "Director General" of this or that. There was a Director General of Telecommunications, a Director General of Roads and Bridges, a Director General of Water, a Director General of Sewage, a Director General of Electricity, a Director General of Agriculture, a Director General of Media, and a Director General of Highways. There was even a Director General of Western Desert Projects. How they came up with the term "Director General," or what it actually meant, was something none of us really could pin down.

Several of the officers of 6th CAG, me included, were assigned with the task of being the liaison for each of the "Director Generals" and to monitor the progress of these Iraqi government officials. I was assigned to "shadow" the Director General of Telecommunication, the Director General of Agriculture, the Director General of Western Desert Projects, and the Director General of Roads and Bridges. Sounds like incredibly hard work but when only four Director Generals would actually show up at the Government Center at any given time, it was not as hard as it might have appeared. In the eight months I was there, I never once saw the Director General of Agriculture; saw the Director General of Western Desert Projects twice; and only saw a picture of the Director General of Roads and Bridges. The Director General of Telecommunications, however, was a gentleman by the name of Engineer Mahmood.

Engineer Mahmoods' full name is something I would prefer to keep to myself, but he was a very handsome and dedicated man. I can say that without fear of being judged in one way or another because I have a few photographs of he and I working together, and everyone has told me he was a handsome man. When I first met him, I was not too sure what to think of him. He spoke and understood quite a bit of English, but he was a hard man to put a finger on as to where he was coming from. His position in Al Anbar Province was one of the most important, but there was something about him when I first met him that seemed timid or meek. I am almost certain that his first impression of me was not favorable at all. I could tell that he was going to be cordial to me, but that is where it was going to end.

Our job as Marines at the Government Center was to keep track of what each "Director General" was doing, what funds he was receiving, and what progress he was making as far as improving the infrastructure of Al Anbar Province. We were then to report to our command what was going on. We were to make a daily report of the progress of our billets. For most of my assignments, it was simple enough. I would report, "Still can't find the sneaky bastard." But not Engineer Mahmood. He was very dedicated and determined to rebuild his country.

It did not take long at the Government Center to find out how dangerous it was for the Iraqis to even be seen with Marines. The unit that had occupied the Government Center before us had hired on a local fourteen-year-old to be a "houseboy." He would help with cleaning during the day and even get some of the local food smuggled in to break up the monotony of MREs, or the food that could survive the long, hot journey in the mail that loved ones from back home would send to their Marines. I do not know the boy's name, but I do know of his fate. He was followed home one evening from the Government Center, kidnapped and beheaded while a video camera captured the gruesome act. Those who committed this barbaric act then had the audacity to come into the lobby of the Government Center (we took great pride that we had such an open door policy) and leave us a copy of the beheading before they slithered out the door. From what I was told, he was a nice and ambitious youth, looking forward to the future of his country that had been given a freedom not even his father could remember.

The repercussions of such an action on the Marines often times makes those who were there lose site of the mission. We too had a "houseboy" by the name of Saad. He was, however, well into his thirties, if not forties, and could not speak. He would occasionally grunt a word or two, but he was clearly not all there. This protected him from those who would otherwise do him harm. It is taboo over there to harm someone who is mentally or physically challenged.

Saad, our "house boy" and Col Burdine.

One time, however, Saad, who would walk three or four miles every day each way to get to the Government Center, was robbed and beaten up by two men. They too had the audacity to enter the Government Center a few days later. Saad simply started shaking uncontrollably at the sight of them. We quickly deduced that these were the men who had made the marks that Saad tried to hide on his face. I, in particular, was mad as hell.

I quickly came up with a plan that would teach these two thugs a lesson in Marine Corps warfare. Most of you are probably thinking that I was planning on going up to them and kicking their asses. I have to admit that this was the first thing that crossed my mind, but we had been indoctrinated in a new type of warfare. It was a chicken-shit type of warfare, which involved hiding behind civilians and not coming out to fight like real soldiers. I was going to give them a taste of their own medicine.

I quickly ran to my rack where my wallet (which I had very little need for at the Government Center) was tucked away with two crisp twenty-dollar bills I had stashed away for emergency purposes. This was just such an emergency. I took those two twenty dollars bills, was going to go up to the two imbeciles who had beat the crap out of Saad, give them a great big hug and a "Salam Alakyum" (Allah be with you), kiss them on both checks and just say, "Shukran, Shukran," which meant, "Thank you, thank you!" Then I was going to stuff the two twenty-dollar bills in their pockets, again thanking them profusely in front of all their Iraqi neighbors. Word would have gotten out within minutes that they were working for the Americans, and thugs much more dangerous than they would have hopefully paid them a little visit that night.

Engineer Mahmood and me after our pack to "Die together."

Unfortunately, they too slithered away by the time I got back to the lobby. I would very much liked to have seen if tapes of them being beheaded ended up in our lobby a few days later. I don't think anyone deserves such a fate, but if you want to be a soldier, fight us like soldiers. We would be more than happy to oblige you.

This and many other incidents made me quickly aware that the Iraqis, like Governor Ma'Moun and Engineer Mahmood, were incredibly brave just coming to the Government Center at all. They also had to keep a distance from us, not just to protect their own lives, but those of their families. I endured many occasions where the Iraqis I worked with would take cheap shots at both the coalition forces and even me personally in front of their peers.

The first time Engineer Mahmood did this to me was in a meeting in front of many of his peers, blaming me for a telecommunication repair that was scheduled but had not been accomplished. It pissed me off to no end. It was in an affluent neighborhood in Ramadi that was not patrolled by our troops, but the telecommunication repairmen had to drive by one of our bases that had a number of tanks. From time to time, the tanks would go on "intimidation runs," which was simply chasing after a random car and scaring the shit out of them.

The telecommunication workers that day were not in the mood for it, so they simply did not show up. I had contacted the tank unit, gave them the description of all the vehicles that would be involved in the repair, so we were good to go.

I was standing right behind Eng Mahmood as he spoke to the group of Director Generals of Al Anbar Province, saying that it was a lack of coordination on the Americans' part (meaning me) that caused the failure of getting telephone lines repaired in a critical part of Ramadi. I stood behind him as he delivered his speech, berating the coalition forces (again, meaning me), and my blood began to boil. He never once turned back to look at me, but I am certain he could feel the back of his head heating up as my stares were boring a hole in his head.

After his theatrical tirade with me standing directly behind him, the Governor of Al Anbar Province, sitting at the head of the long oval-shaped conference table, looked directly at me and knowing that I was pissed, asked me what I thought about the failed mission. I will freely admit that my gut instinct was to say, "It sure as hell wasn't my fault," but I knew deep down that crying like a baby was going to get absolutely nothing accomplished. I swallowed my pride and simply said, "We will do better next time," then I quickly bit my tongue so the words that really wanted to come out would have to get by the blood that was seeping from my tongue.

I sat down after Engineer Mahmood had finished his speech, and another Director General gave his speech in front of his peers, but I was not listening. I was still fuming. I was really upset that someone whom I had grown to like and respect had dimed me out. I did not want to have anything to do with any of these theatrical bastards. When the meeting came to a close, rather than doing the customary thank you and handshakes, without so much as a word, I gathered my gear, put it on and started briskly to my quarters.

As I was walking down the hallway to the courtyard, Engineer Mahmood came after me. I ignored his shouts of, "Lt. Legge, Lt. Legge," and kept up my brisk pace. He must have gone into a run because he caught me before I got to the exit. He grabbed me by the shoulder, turned me towards him, looked me in the eyes and without a single word being spoken in either Arabic or English, we came to an agreement at that moment. He apologized without saying a word and I in turn understood why he did what he did.

After that single moment in time, we were heading in the right direction.

CHAPTER TWELVE

JULY 2004
CRAWFORD, TEXAS

I hesitate to tell this part of the tale, but quite frankly it is just too funny and stupid not to tell. It started out very innocently. It was a Sunday morning and I had the TV on CNN as I was doing laundry so that I would have something to wear for church. I was folding clothes, which usually takes my complete attention, and I overheard a news report of the President being at his Crawford, Texas ranch where he was going to do his regular three-mile run. They said those who braved the Texas heat and ran with him actually got a t-shirt that said something like "I survived the Crawford Run" or something like that.

Now, Crawford is only two hours south of where I live and it is on the way to College Station where my oldest daughter was attending Texas A&M. I had no children with me that day, had nothing really planned for the day.... what the heck. Road trip! I want to make it perfectly clear at this juncture of this story that I had absolutely no aspirations of going down to Crawford, knocking on the door of the Crawford Ranch and asking if George wanted to come out and play. At best, I thought there might be some press personnel who followed the President and a hundred or so secret servicemen at least a mile behind.

The drive to Crawford was uneventful and time passed quickly. I thought this would be a great opportunity to actually time my three-mile run. It would not be official, but I thought I would at least have a starter and someone could time me at the finish. As I came into the town of Crawford, there was little to no difference between this tiny Texas town and hundreds of other one-gas-station towns that spot the Texas plains. I pulled into the one gas station and asked if they knew where the press headquartered. As most in Texas do when you ask them for directions, the nice gentleman walked out of the gas station and pointed down the road. "Ya go down there to that big oak tree, ya take a right, ya go about two miles and ya just can't miss it."

I thanked him for the directions and went to the big oak tree, took a right and went about two miles. Sure enough, there was a state trooper's car in the middle of the road. As I slowly approached, a very large state trooper got out of his air-conditioned vehicle and stepped onto the hot Texas pavement. I stopped and rolled down my window. About that time, the passenger door of the trooper's car opened and an even larger gentleman got out. He, however, was wearing a suit and tie. He also left the comfort of his air-conditioned ride. Obviously, secret service. I just had no idea they grew them that big.

The state trooper came up to my window and asked if there is anything he could help me with. The secret serviceman was in the background, waiting to hear my response. "Well sir, this may sound crazy, but I heard something on CNN this morning about a presidential run, and they were even giving away t-shirts." I tried to keep it light, just in case I was way off base on this run. The secret serviceman then stepped up to the car and said, "You are here to do what?" I explained that I had just overheard something on the news about the President running a three-mile run and those who participated in the run got a t-shirt.

The state trooper asked for my license, which I quickly gave him, and I was beginning to think this was not one of the most brilliant ideas I had ever come up with. I said, "If I am way off base on this run thing, I will get out of your way post haste." The state trooper and the secret serviceman were both looking at my license and neither responded to my statement. I said again, this time directed to the secret serviceman, "If I am causing a problem here, I am sorry and will just move on." He said something like, "No problem at all, just wait here."

He went back to the state trooper's vehicle and got on the radio. I thought, cool, I might just get to run after all. He came back from making his call, smiled at me and said, "It will just be one minute, sir." I said, "Thanks, I appreciate it." I was beginning to stretch my legs a little bit, preparing for what I was certain to be at least a twenty-minute three mile run, when over the horizon, on this small Texas road, side-by-side, came roaring three black SUV's. They came to screeching stop just yards away from my car. They did not jump out. Instead, they opened their doors and just unwound out of each vehicle, each larger than the one before him.

I wasn't going to get to run with the President, was I?

As my car was being surrounded by these large gentlemen, it appeared as if they were deciding on who got to mess with this one. One of the smaller secret servicemen finally seemed to have been chosen. He was only 6'3" and around 225 lbs. He bent over to have a peek at me and said, "Could you please step out of the car?" Everyone knows what it is liked to be stopped by the police and some know what it is like to be asked to step out of the car. I'll bet there aren't many who get to say they had to step out of a car amongst seven secret servicemen and a state trooper.

I can't even begin to remember all the questions I was asked over the next forty-five minutes. It would be easier to tell what they didn't ask. The only thing that comes to mind is they did not ask if I had ever read "Mein Kampf." They asked me who I was, who I knew, who I didn't know, who I wanted to know. They searched my car and even went through my golf bag. They made fun of my putter. I won a putter in a golf tournament years ago that is the same putter that Jack Nicklaus won the 1986 Masters with. It is, however, a very large putter. Every time I golf with someone for the first time, I get ribbed about the size of my "stereo speakers!" By the end of the round, however, they are usually much less vocal because one thing I can do is putt.

Now I had seven secret servicemen making fun of my putter! This, however, was not the worst part of this debacle. Of the many questions they asked, one was if I had any military experience. I explained that I did and that I was currently putting my package in to get back into the Marine Corps. This in no way helped my cause. At this point, they were certain that I was nuts. One of the secret servicemen asked, "Why is someone your age, who owns his own company, trying to get back into the Marine Corps?"

"That is a darn good question" I thought. When they found out that I had been turned down once, they said, "Well you need to take a no as a no."

Just when I thought it could not get any worse, they asked for phone numbers of someone who could vouch for me. One person they wanted to telephone was LtCol Ingalls, but lucky for me it was Sunday and she could not be reached. They did get hold of my daughter at Texas A&M. I had explained to them that I was going to stop in and take her to dinner on my little road trip. They simply could not get over the fact that I would drive two hours to go for a three-mile run.

After suffering a little more abuse from them, trying to see if I would blow a fuse, they let me go. They sent me off with a two car escort that followed me all the way back to the interstate and several miles on it, making certain I was not going to turn around and ask George if he wanted to go golfing.

About ten minutes later, my cell phone rang. It is my daughter at A&M. All she could say was, "Daddy, what have you done?!"

CHAPTER THIRTEEN

JULY 2004
BEDFORD, TEXAS

When I returned home, back where I belonged, I was certain that my little road trip had ended my chances of being brought back into the Marine Corps. The first thing I did was call LtCol Ingalls and explained what I had done. All she did was laugh. It was a great relief to me that she had thought it was funny. LtCol Ingalls had been one of the Marines stationed at the White House during the Clinton Administration and was aware of how the secret service operated. She said that they were just messing with me and there was probably no formal record of the incident.

Just to be certain, the next day I called the Secret Service branch in Austin, the nearest branch to Crawford, and introduced myself as the idiot who wanted to run with the President the previous day. There was an immediate muffled laugh at the other end of the phone. They knew who I was. I explained my circumstance of having a package sent to headquarters Marine Corps and that if this was going to be part of my official record, I needed to know so as to either pull my package for consideration or at least be prepared to explain the incident. Again, a muffled laugh. The female secret service agent on the other end of the phone simply said, "Our agents in Crawford don't actually see much action down there. You broke up what was otherwise going to be a really boring day."

In a way, I was relieved. Yet in another way, I felt like I needed a shower after being used by the Secret Service. One way or the other made no difference. My package was going to go forward once again. I took my simulated PFT myself and did rather well. I ran three miles in just under twenty-one minutes (not as good as I had hoped, but very reputable), did 80 sit-ups and managed to do twelve pull-ups in spite of a still-injured shoulder. LtCol Ingalls spent an enormous amount of her personal time getting my package just perfect. I will never be able to thank her enough for the effort she put into getting me back into the Corps.

While my package was being prepared for the second time, the least I could do was to help with the Marine Corps Toys for Tots campaign. It is surprising how few people realize that the Toys for Tots campaign is run by the Marine Corps Reserve program, and even fewer realize what goes into the campaign. Toys for Tots is one of the very few charitable organizations where virtually all of the toys, and especially money, donated to the campaign actually go where it is supposed to go, to families in need. Some large charitable organizations only give fifty to sixty percent to their cause, the rest of the money goes to running the organization and advertising. Ninety seven percent of Toys for Tots donations goes directly towards buying toys, which are directly distributed, to kids who, on Christmas morning, would otherwise go without. It was a great cause and drained the resources of the reserve units, so I was prepared to help out.

I was introduced to the coordinator and over the next three months, spent more time at the Toys for Tots warehouse than I did at my office, home, or the two combined. Luckily, my children got involved as well, especially my then-four-year-old son. He got a big kick out of being in the warehouse with not only a huge amount of toys, but also Marines in uniform who adopted him as their mascot. If Joshua got out of line, the Marines would simply throw him in one of the large packing boxes where he had no way of getting out which he thought was the greatest thing ever. I was beginning to feel like I was back in the Corps. Being around Marines again was a good feeling. This would not last for long.

It did not take headquarters long to respond. This letter did not have the same cordial attitude as the first. Instead of saying thank you for your interest in getting back into the Corps, the tone was more like "we told you that you could not get back in the Corps, so stop bothering us." I was much more prepared for this rejection than the first. I resigned myself to the fact that working for the Toys for Tots campaign not only helped the Marine Corps, but also brightened Christmas morning for over one hundred thousand children in the Dallas/Fort Worth metroplex. I was disappointed, but happy that at least I was giving something back.

I submersed myself in the campaign. I was putting at least fifty hours a week into the campaign and had one of my administrative assistants, Julia Fisher, working full-time for the campaign. I would like to say that I did most of the work, but when I decided to write this book, I swore that I would be as accurate as possible. I can tell a pretty good story, just ask my kids. So, truth be told, Julia was the go-to person. When we needed to get something donated to the campaign, like food, tape, boxes, furniture, heaters, RV's, propane, warehouse space, trucks, telephone service, electricity, paper, copiers, computers, dumpsters, Internet services or eight thousand other little things, Julia got the job done. Of course, as any good officer in the Corps would do, I took full credit for it. This made me look like a champion.

General Bill Gossell, a retired Major General in the Marine Corps who had for many years dedicated his life to doing volunteer work for Toys for Tots, noticed the contribution that "I" made. Major General Gossell is one of the most generous individuals I have ever met in my life. The amount of time he puts in year-round for the Toys for Tots campaign makes the Dallas/Fort Worth Toys for Tots campaign the largest in the country. He also was a close friend with Lieutenant General John Bergman, head of the Reserve Affair Division of the Marine Corps at the time. When Major General Gossell heard that I had been turned down, he made a call to his friend. I was granted an interview with Lt. General Bergman, head of the reserves in Quantico, Virginia.

I thought this was probably another chance for a huge disappointment, but I decided I was going to go into this with nothing but a positive attitude. I made the call to Quantico, talked to the Lt. General's aide and set an interview for the following week. I booked my flight to DC and said a quick prayer.

I arrived in DC the night before the meeting. I was not going to be late for this interview. The drive down to Quantico reminded me of the time many years ago that I had driven back to Quantico after my few hours spent with my wife. This time, I was going to fight to get back into the Marine Corps, not to get out.

When I arrived, I was introduced to a Colonel who already had the two previous packages that had been sent to headquarters, along with a bunch of paperwork, which I still have no idea the contents of. She was familiar with who I was and talked with me for several minutes while Lt. General Bergman was on an important phone call. I have to admit that I was rather nervous. Generals are not exactly the kind of officers who an ordinary Marine spent much time around.

As the Colonel and I were exchanging pleasantries, Lt. General Bergman's door opened. He came out with a smile and said, "So, you are Lt. Legge." Just being called Lt. Legge again, especially by a General, was well worth the trip. He invited me into his office. I went in, trying to maintain what little military bearing I could remember from so many years ago. He was a very charismatic and friendly man. He asked me several basic questions such as how I got into the Corps and where I had been stationed while in the Corps.

It just so happened that the LtCol I had worked for at HT-18, the advanced helicopter training squadron, twenty years ago, LtCol Jack Wagner, was a good friend of his.

Lt. Col. Wagner was, of all things, a great badminton player. The Commanding Officer of HT-8, the other helicopter squadron, just happened to also be an outstanding badminton player. I know what most of you are thinking. Marines… playing badminton? I too, at the time, thought that this was not exactly a macho sport. I had played a little tennis at the University of Oklahoma, and Lt. Col. Wagner wanted to win the Captains Cup in badminton in Pensacola that year. He recruited me. The first time we played, I learned quickly that this is an exhausting sport. We won the Captains cup that year, by the way. Enough of this macho sports stuff, back to the story.

Lt. General Bergman got straight to the point. He explained that the only reason he was meeting with me was because they were forming a brand new CAG to be deployed to Iraq in only a few months. He stopped, stared at me, and asked me point blank, "Are you willing to give up at least a year of your life and go to a combat zone?" Without hesitation, I said, "Yes, sir."

As soon as I had left the building where what seemed to be the place where they were going to take a chance on an old Lt, I got out my cell phone. I called a Major I knew in the Marine Corps and told him that it appeared as though I was being brought back in the Corps.

"Just one thing Major" I just had to ask. "What is a CAG?"

Seemingly perplexed, he responded, "It is a Carrier Air Group. Why?"

"They seem to want me to help start up a new CAG. The General said they needed Marines that could think outside of the box."

The major was a fighter pilot and I am sure he thought I was nuts, but he said nothing. For five days I was telling everyone that I was going to be involved in setting up a new Carrier Air Group. Maybe they thought that my limited time in flight school would give me something of an edge in this monumental undertaking.

LtCol Ingalls was out of town at the time, but upon her return she gave me a call and asked how my meeting had gone.

"Ma'am, you will not believe this but they are bringing me back to help set up a new Carrier Air Group" I said.

"What?" was her only response.

"They are starting up a new CAG and the General thought I might be of help" I said, knowing something was up.

"CAG does not stand for Carrier Air Group (she did not actually say idiot, but it was implied) it is a Civil Affairs Group."

After our brief conversation came to an end, I immediately called the Major that had informed me that CAG stood for Carrier Air Group, and said

"Sir, CAG apparently does not stand for Carrier Air Group but Civil Affairs Group. What the heck is that and what will I be doing."

There was a long pause, and the entire Major said was "You are going to get shot at. You are going to get shot at a lot."

I had no idea at the time how right he would be.

CHAPTER FOURTEEN

SEPTEMBER 2005
THE GOVERNMENT CENTER, RAMADI, IRAQ

Shortly after Engineer Mahmood and I came to our silent agreement, we got the minor telecommunication repair done in the affluent neighborhood of Ramadi and Eng. Mahmood was very happy with the results. Not only did many wealthy have phone service once again, but also I think there might have been a bonus for Eng. Mahmood in some way or another. This was just the forward momentum I was looking for. I took advantage of the positive attitude he and his workers displayed and asked, "What's next?"

Engineer Mahmood said that what he really wanted to get up and running was the fiber optic line. It was a fiber-optic telecommunications line that ran from the Syrian border all the way to Baghdad. It was a state-of-the-art communication line, which, at the time, not even the Americans had much experience with. It was a source of pride for the Iraqis and especially Eng. Mahmood. He was a very intelligent man and wanted to show the world they were on the cutting edge of technology. The only problem was that this fiber-optic line ran directly down Route Michigan, the most bombed road in all of Iraq.

The line had been hit by so many IEDs that it had never actually functioned from Syria to Baghdad. The area in which the line had been diagnosed as broken was a notoriously bad place. It was out in the desert, which offered no protection for anyone working on the roadside, and rumor had it there was a Syrian sniper who had taken over one of the few houses that dotted the desert. I had even heard rumors that it was a husband and wife team, and they were incredibly accurate. I have no facts to back that up, but it made for an interesting story at the time.

This part of Iraq was also very bad for both sides. Two Marines had just been killed days earlier in the area where we were to make the repairs. I arrived at the conclusion that an IED had broken the line and killed the two Marines. Iraqi workers who had worked in the area were killed as well by the indiscriminate insurgents who could care less who they killed. This repair was not going to be a cakewalk by any means for either side, but for some reason, both Eng. Mahmood and I were determined to get this repair done. Not only were we determined, I said that I was going out there personally and not just coordinating it from the sidelines as I had with a few repairs earlier. Eng. Mahmood was not as enthusiastic about going on the repair as I was, but you could tell that he was not going to let me get credit for something he wanted so badly. On the day we were set to make the repair, Eng. Mahmood was going along for the ride.

One of the most important parts of my job, in addition to shadowing Director Generals who were making repairs to the infrastructure of Iraq, was something we called "deconfliction." Now, the word deconfliction is not in the dictionary, although from what I have heard, it has been around for quite some time. It is a term used in warfare when we do our best to avoid a conflict. This entails informing two adversarial sides what the other side is doing so as to avoid bloodshed. This ends up being much more time consuming than you might imagine.

Me giving a lecture to the Iraqis on the importance of deconfliction.

The most critical part of a deconfliction is letting every weapon-possessing person in the area you are working, or will be traveling to in order to get to the repair, know exactly what is going to happen. We have young Marines stationed everywhere who have acutely narrow fields of responsibilities that they take very seriously. If something out of the ordinary happens in their field of fire, which can be as simple as an automobile stopping, there is no telling how they might react. Letting them know in advance exactly who to expect and what is going to happen brings down the tension level and makes for a much safer working environment. But this means letting everyone in the area know you plan to work in their area of operation and don't shoot if you see some digging.

This particular repair involved so many units, spread over such a wide area, that just finding which units needed to be briefed was quite an undertaking. I spent several days on the phone, contacting each unit to see what they could offer for support and what we needed to do to make their mission easier. There were Army units involved, both ground and air, as well as countless Marine units that would not only be at the site of the repair, but units who would protect us on the fifteen mile route to the repair. It was much like a relay race with us being the baton handed from unit to unit.

Although this was a very important mission for me, it was not my only responsibility. I had to go to Baghdad just prior to this mission for an agricultural conference that I had committed to weeks earlier. To me, getting the economic stability back to the Iraqis was key to making this mission a success, and agriculture was one of the primary goals. I hesitate to put this in this book for the fact that it might lessen credibility, as well as having those reading this come to the incontrovertible conclusion that I am just plain nuts, but I just have to include it. The conference that I was going to attend was not only about ideas on how to get the agriculture back to its former self, but to explore the opportunities for tourism as well. I just had to hear what they planned for tourists.

Before the conference, I felt pretty confident that I had covered all my bases. Although I was just a lowly 1st Lt., I think my age was becoming known amongst the other units in the area so I was given a little more leeway in trying to set up unusual missions. The Army unit commanders were also very helpful and cooperative in lending their support. Everyone was on board, the times for all units were set, all memos had gone out detailing the plan- units involved, Iraqi vehicles that would be involved down to specifics of their color and license plate numbers, number of workers in each vehicle as well as what they would be wearing. The only thing we were lacking was the exact coordinate of where the dig would take place. From what I was told by Eng. Mahmood, they simply had to tap into the fiber-optic line close to the

Government Center, send out some sort of beam of light that would travel to where the break occurred, then send back the data they needed to determine exactly where the break existed. I did not understand, but it seemed like this would be a no-brainer. I left for the conference in Baghdad confident that there were no worries.

CHAPTER FIFTEEN

OCTOBER 2005
BAGHDAD, IRAQ

Normally, soldiers who are in a war zone are not allowed to divulge their whereabouts or where they are traveling, but as Civil Affairs Marines, our work was somewhat different. Having people know what we were accomplishing and when we were accomplishing it was part of our unwritten mission. With this in mind, the several trips I made to Baghdad for economic development and other things I saw, I had no problem in letting my family back home know about. This turned out to be a great mistake and reason for much laughter with them upon my return home. Every time I went to Baghdad, I let them know where I would be, and that I would probably be unable to touch base with them for a while, either due to travel time getting to Baghdad or the lack of ability getting to a computer or phone once I was there.

Although there were plenty of phones in the Green Zone at the Embassy in Baghdad, my stays in Baghdad were ones that I simply wanted to get in and out of. I felt guilty about being there while my unit was under constant attack of some sort or another. My family, on the other hand, would send desperate messages to me when they knew that I was in Baghdad, begging me to tell them when I had returned back to Ramadi where they had grown accustomed to believing that I was safe. We have laughed many times about the irony of those times they thought that my being in Baghdad meant trouble and that Ramadi was home.

Front of the United States Embassy in the Green Zone, Baghdad, Iraq.

Baghdad Pool behind the Embassy.

The truth is, at the time, the Green Zone was like an oasis compared to those who were in outposts. There was a pool people could sit around with absolutely no armor or weapons. There was karaoke on Wednesday, pool tables in a lovely gazebo, ping-pong tables and even alcohol. There were also women. Real women. Women who not only wore real people clothes but smelled good. Surrounding the pool were signs that said, "No drinking while armed." No shit.

For those who are not aware, as Marines, we were forbidden both women and alcohol for our deployment in Iraq. Although I did not miss the alcohol at all, I grew an even greater admiration for the opposite sex that I will never take for granted again.

But this sign that said, "No drinking while armed," to me typified what was going on in Baghdad so I simply had to make fun of it. I found the most beautiful woman in the green zone and convinced her to pose with me for a picture in front of the sign. I took my 9mm pistol that I carried with me at all times that was connected to my holster with a spring-like cord, handed it to this lovely young lady and held up an O'Doul's beer can in one hand as the other arm was wrapped around the waist of this Baghdad Goddess. Someone was kind enough to take the picture that I was determined to bring back to my troops and torment them- "Did he or didn't he?"

I did not, by the way. Toughest decision I made the entire tour.

Not at all what it appears to be.

The conference was pretty much what I expected. They had absolutely no clue about what was going on outside the walls of the Green Zone. There were so many well-intentioned people who sacrificed their time and risked their lives trying to get something accomplished in Iraq. But, no matter how many times they were told not to do things the American way and to instead think about how the Iraqis were used to doing things, it was something they simply could not understand due to being tucked away in the safe walls of the Green Zone.

One issue I was eager to explore was advancing the cultivation of dates back into Iraq. I had done some research and was surprised to find that Iraq, at one time, had produced a third of the world's dates. Agriculture, though you would not expect in a country primarily landscaped by deserts, used to be a very significant percentage of Iraq's Gross National Product. I had always thought that oil was their only revenue. It became clear to me that just getting the agricultural output up to even half of what it was capable of would make an enormous difference in their economy.

After a long lecture on this and that - tourism was only briefly touched on, I assume because someone must have shown them pictures of the real Iraq - there was a question and answer session. I asked what was being done in the area of date production. The narrator informed me that they had looked into cultivating dates but determined it too labor intensive and therefore not economically viable. He quickly went to the next question. After a few more questions were entertained, I raised my hand again. I repeated the idea of date cultivation and cited that at one time, dates had been a staple of their agricultural economy. I was again quickly put in my place and told that there were many more agricultural avenues to be pursued which would prove much more profitable. This time I could tell the narrator was a bit irritated with my persistence.

I certainly do not blame the narrator for not understanding my mission, nor do many Americans truly understand just how little the average Iraqi needs to survive. It has been determined that the average Iraqi lives on around $100 per month. Take that $100 away from him and he can no longer feed his family. That is where the insurgency wanted him. They would offer him $100 just to shoot at the Government Center with an AK47, $1,000 for sending a 60mm mortar into the Government Center, and $10,000 if they could destroy one of our humvees with an IED and get it on tape.

I have really tried to keep my "opinion" out of this book, but it just seems to me that if you allow a man to feed his family, you will not have a problem with him. Take that away and even I don't know what I would do.

After what seemed like the end of the questions, my hand went up again. I could tell the narrator was not interested in answering another question from the "date guy," but I was determined. The narrator reluctantly recognized me, and I tried to explain that labor-intensive projects were exactly what we were trying to find in Al Anbar Province. I explained that we were trying to get as many MAMs (military-aged males) as possible any kind of work so that they might stop shooting at us. When the narrator heard that I was from Al Anbar Province, I could tell his attitude quickly changed. He listened to my stories, including our giving MAMs even menial jobs such as cleaning up the decimated streets of Ramadi, which considerably cut down the amount of attacks we received at night and which also seemed to bring back a pride in the residents with whom we came into contact.

We talked a bit more about various things regarding agriculture such as the spraying of crops, seed cleaners and the tractor program that had been set up to repair some of the dilapidated tractors the farmers had in Iraq. I quickly asked if there was any money left in the tractor program that we could take back to the farmers in Al Anbar Province, but was told that that money had run out. By this time, I was getting a bit cocky. My hand went up again. "You mean there is no more money left to repair tractors?" The response was "No." Without raising my hand, I replied, "What if we shoot them?" The narrator looked at me not understanding what I was saying and said, "You are going to shoot the farmers?" I said, "No, just their tractors."

According to the rules set up for reparations, we were allowed to pay up to $2,500 per "accidental" shooting when we happened to destroy property. What would the consequences be if we were to "accidentally" shoot a few tractors? Could we have them repaired by the group that had been organized to repair tractors in this program? The narrator was not sure what could be done in that set of circumstances or what the hell I was getting at. He did, however, want to give me something I could take back and told me they had a great program of seed cleaners that still had funds.

A seed cleaner is a relatively simple machine that is used to clean food-crop seeds of excess dirt and debris. It was determined that the output of productivity would increase yield of the crop by 25 percent. The machines were only around $16,000 and portable. I thought we could get one for Al Anbar Province and take it from farmer to farmer to increase their productivity. It was at least some progress or was it?

After the conference, I asked a few more questions. I knew that the Director General in charge of Food Distribution would not allow any outside seeds coming from foreign sources wanting to keep things in-house, so-to-speak. I also learned that he had no interest in these seed cleaners. When asking if the seed cleaners would help a farmer who already had ten bags of dirty seeds to increase his productivity, they did not have an answer. It turned out that the local farmer would end up with seven and a half bags of seeds rather than the ten bags he was accustomed to. This program, although filled with good intentions, would ultimately piss off the farmer rather than make him feel as though we were helping.

I was anxious to leave the conference and get back to fixing the fiber optic line. That, at least, was something you could see the results of.

CHAPTER SIXTEEN

OCTOBER 2005
THE GOVERNMENT CENTER, RAMADI, IRAQ

When I returned to the safety of the Government Center (I get such a kick out of that), I had to turn right around and head to Habbaniyah, another hot spot in Iraq, where we were going to meet the Iraqi telecommunication workers for the fiber- optic repair. I was given the coordinates where the repair was to take place by my new XO at the Government Center. I did not know it at the time, but it was the exact eight-digit coordinate where two Marines had been killed just days prior. When I arrived in Habbaniyah, they were making preparations for the services of these two Marines. The services, however, were going to take place the next day, the day we were to make the repairs.

I was torn as what to do. I did not want to take soldiers away from a service of their fallen friends, but at the same time, extensive preparations had been made and so many units were ready to go. I spoke briefly with a Marine in Habbiniyah and asked him if we should postpone the mission. He looked tired and distant but did not hesitate in his answer, "We move on."

One of the major problems I could not overcome in my original preparations was that I could not get the Iraqis to go in a convoy with the coalition forces from the Government Center to Habbiniyah, nor could I convince them to meet us at the base at Habbiniyah. They insisted we meet them at the repair site where we could then provide them security. This may not sound like a problem, but if I had a dime for every hour I waited for a single Iraqi to show up at a scheduled meeting at the Government Center, I would be a rich man.

The chance of getting eight Iraqis together and to a very dangerous place, all on time, was simply an impossibility. On the behalf of the Iraqis, they would often be stuck in their homes due to maneuvers in the area or would be caught in an unexpected roadblock we might have set up as a random checkpoint.

Two things I was absolutely certain of: one, we were supposed to meet the workers at 0900, and two they would not be there at 0900. Marines don't like to hear that. The Army was not too thrilled either. The idea of sitting out in a very open area of Route Michigan with a hill on one side that overlooked where we would be working would make us feel like sitting ducks.

Everyone agreed that sitting out there for a few minutes, let alone hours, was not a great idea. Also, we could not just wait at the base and leave once our drones in the air spotted the workers. We opted to gather at a bridge not far from the main gate of the camp at Habbiniyah where we had overhead support on top of the bridge.

We got our gear, a full battle load of ammo and went to the assembly area under the bridge, assembling at 0745 (which is 0800 for Marines), just in case the mission started early. This was clearly not my idea and done against my recommendation of nineish. Marines don't like times that end in -ish, even if going to cocktail hour. Needless to say, the workers did not show up early.

Nine o'clock rolled around and still no workers. This was not unexpected but we were all starting to get prepared to pull out and travel the mile to the location of the workers.

Ten o'clock came and went and you could feel the tension in the air. We had five up-armored humvees in my direct unit and had dozens of vehicles protecting us, ranging from other humvees to tanks that would roar by from time to time, chasing off any vehicles that looked at all suspicious. Only a quarter mile down the road was a taxi stand. It looked so odd to see dozens of taxis coming in and out but life had to go on for Iraqis regardless of what the coalition forces had on their minds.

By eleven o'clock, just about everyone was getting pissed off. Because I had instigated this mission, I was getting more and more stares. Commanders of various units were either calling me on the radio or were rolling by in tanks asking the old Lt., "What the hell is going on?" Things were just a bit tense.

We had now been sitting under the bridge for over three hours. We had various assets watching the site where the workers were supposed to show up, but no workers. The only excitement that we had all morning was when the post on top of the bridge opened fire with his 50 cal machine gun, letting out five or six bursts of twenty to thirty rounds. There was a thirty second pause, then five or six more bursts. We all assumed our defensive positions, which we had gone over for several hours in our pre-convoy brief, but we had no idea which way to defend. I could hear the frantic voice traffic over the radio with commander after commander trying to get in touch with whoever was doing the firing. After a minute or two of confusion, finally someone seemed to be in touch with the post that was above us.

"What the hell is going on up there?" shouted one Marine to another.

There was a garbled response that no one could understand, followed by another quick burst of rounds. By this time we could at least identify which direction the rounds were being sent.

Again someone called out, "What the hell are you shooting at?"

Again a garbled response but I could definitely pick up the word "squatting."

"Did you say squatting?" was the reply of the Commander readying his troops for a frontal assault.

"Yeah, this guy keeps squatting over there by the gas station," was the now clear response of the machine gunner.

"Say that again?" shouted the stunned Commander.

"I say I have an Iraqi in my field of fire that keeps squatting by the gas pumps directly west of my position," stated the very calm gunner.

One more very quick burst of rounds was sent in the direction of that poor Iraqi that literally got caught with his pants down, and we all had a good laugh. Nothing happened to the Iraqi gentleman, but he was forced to move several times. I find it amazing the things the Iraqis have learned to adapt to.

By noon, there was not a happy camper to be found. Although we had not received any fire all morning, everyone was growing tired of waiting. I managed to keep the units there till just after one in the afternoon, but the mission was officially called off at about 1315. I don't think anyone spoke to me for at least an hour. We went back to the camp at Habbiniyah where I am sure everyone was debating who was going to have the privilege of chewing out the 1st Lt. from the CAG unit.

I took it like a man although it was not that much of a chewing out. What made me feel the worst was that I had wasted the time of many, many individuals, and had put them in harm's way for no reason.

I also heard an earful of just how much I had cost the American taxpayer. I think someone came up with the cost of $400,000 that had just been flushed down the toilet for a completely wasted mission. For all you taxpayers, I am truly sorry. I am doing my best to repay it.

When I got back to the Government Center, I had several calls to make to units that wanted to know what the hell had gone wrong. Before I made a call, my own unit wanted to know what had gone wrong. This event was an embarrassment for our unit and made us look incompetent. We had involved many units and all of them wanted to know where the foul up was. Eng. Mahmood had already been to the Government Center prior to my return and said that no one was at the location for the repair. When they stopped to just do the repair by themselves, a single tank ran them off.

I knew this could not be the case because I had been in constant contact with the units that were watching the area and this clearly would have been reported to me. I first called the Tank Unit that had been covering us and asked them if there was any way this could have accidentally happened. I am sure the Commander of the unit thought I was just trying to get out of the blame, but he checked with each of his tank Commanders and got back to me quickly, stating emphatically that there was absolutely no way any of his tanks were involved in anything like this.

I then had to assume that Eng. Mahmood was lying to me, but this just never really sank in. I knew he was not lying to me. There had to be some other explanation. I called Eng. Mahmood at home. This was something I avoided doing as much as possible because I did not want him to start avoiding any of my calls, as so many of the Director Generals did with their Marine counterparts. I tried not to use interpreters when I made such calls so that he knew it was me who wanted to talk to him.

His wife, who spoke very little English, answered the phone, and I greeted her with, "As-sallaammu-alaykum," the formal greeting in Iraq, and she responded with, "Wa-alaykum-assalam."

"Ann eazinak," was my next forced phrase in Arabic which meant, "excuse me," and I asked to speak to Eng. Mahmood. I could tell from the tone of her voice that although she did not like having a Marine calling her home and putting her and her family in danger for working with us, she did, however speak with a tone of respect for me that clearly her husband had conveyed to her.

When Eng. Mahmood came to the phone, all I could ask him was, "What happened today?" He told me the same story that my unit told me earlier. He said that he and his workers had gone to the site and waited on us to arrive for "many minutes." When we did not show up, they got out and started unloading their equipment, and a tank came storming up and "shot" at them.

I did not know what to think. It was not at all uncommon for Iraqi workers to simply change their minds because they did not feel comfortable about the situation, deciding it was not worth the risk. They would just turn around at the first sight of troops and call it a day. I would not have blamed Eng. Mahmood for doing that exact thing if one of our tanks had intimidated him and his workers, but the units had said nothing about such an incident.

After rechecking with all his tanks, the Unit Commander told me nothing of the sort had occurred. I was between a rock and a hard place.

I reported back to my XO that it was my opinion Eng. Mahmood was not lying and that there had to be some other explanation. I was again berated for not having accomplished the mission, for having embarrassed the unit and questioning the word of a higher-ranking officer. I explained that in no way was I questioning the word of anyone in any of the units there that day. There just had to be another explanation. When asked what that explanation could possibly be, I could only answer with, "I have no idea."

Marines don't like, "I have no idea."

Engineer Mahmood and I sat down the next day and went over the grid coordinates, just as he had done with the XO, and with no hesitancy pointed to the spot where the repair needed to be done. Sure enough, it was two and a half miles from where we were originally told it was. I still can't figure out how we got the exact eight digit grid coordinates of where those Marines had been killed, according to our significant events report.

CHAPTER SEVENTEEN

OCTOBER 2005
THE GOVERNMENT CENTER, RAMADI, IRAQ

I began calling the other units to get the mission set up again. I sent my plans to everyone involved, including all the details of our movements, along with the new eight digit grid coordinates. Some units were not affected by the coordinates where the repair was going to take place because they were only involved in providing protection through their area of operations, so I received little to no backlash from them. Those that were involved in the final repair site, especially the new unit where the repair was now to take place and the other unit that had been informed previously it was in their AO, were not too happy. Word got out that there had been a fuck-up and everyone wanted to jump on the Old Lt., including my own unit.

Most of those involved just got a kick out of pointing out that the fuck-up had been made. I think it made them feel better about lashings they received somewhere in their past. It is somehow tied to our basic instinct to laugh when someone falls down. A few others involved, however, simply would not let this screw-up go away.

"How in the hell could you miss an eight digit coordinate by two miles?!" was the most common question I would get from my superiors.

On a conference call with several units and various commanders ranking from Captain on up to full Bird Colonel to try and get the mission back on track, one officer in particular kept going back to the fact that the first mission's coordinates were no where near these new coordinates.

He just kept asking how this could have happened (knowing full well what he thought the answer was). We were getting nowhere because the discussion kept returning to this. I finally interrupted and said, "The wrong coordinates were completely my responsibility. I guess the time lapse of twenty years between navigation classes was something I should have taken into consideration." I said this with no sense of humor, just as direct a statement as I could possibly make. Someone came back with something like, "Hell of a mistake to make with so many troops involved."

I replied with, "Yes sir, not something I take lightly either."

There were a few more comments made, but most involved were just ready to get on with things. The goat had been castrated, and it was time to get down to business. We continued with the new plans and a new date was set. It was time for round two.

In the days prior to the mission, I felt confident that we would get the repair done this time. I really did not have any thoughts of, "What if this mission fails as well?" Either I did not care, or I was so confident that everything had been planned down to the last detail, that there was no way failure was even an option. I had since worked out a few of the problems with the previous mission, such as having to wait at the end of the route where the repair was going to take place. I arranged with Eng. Mahmood to call me from the telecommunications building, only a few blocks from the Government Center where his workers were going to meet and depart from. As soon as they left, our troops already set up in the courtyard of the Government Center would follow behind at a safe distance and meet up with them around a mile outside of town, avoiding the appearance of the workers being with our convoy. They had made that desire very clear. They did not want tanks following or leading them in downtown Ramadi.

Everyone was in agreement. We could then contact each of the units along the route as we approached so that they could position themselves where needed. The day of the repair came and everyone was where they were supposed to be. My unit was ready in the courtyard, engines running, prepared for anything. I sat by the phone waiting on a call that he had promised would come by 0900. By 0905, I have to admit; my butt cheeks were a bit clenched. The Government Center was swarming with other Marines who had business there that day and they knew this was Round Two. The Marines who had been part of the five-hour wait-a-thon a week earlier were taking bets as to whether the Iraqis would show or no-show.

As I was sitting in the communication room, waiting on the phone to ring, I heard from down the hallway, "Lt. Legge," in a voice that I had come to recognize instantly. It was Eng. Mahmood. He was not supposed to be here. "Eng. Mahmood, what are you doing here?" was all I could say. "We go fix fiber optic line today. You say nine, it is nine!"

"I thought you were going to call me when you were leaving and we would meet outside of town?" "We meet you at repair, OK?" said Eng. Mahmood.

By this time, the commander of the unit that was heading up the convoy from the Government Center and his Staff Sgt. were standing in the hallway, along with my CO and XO, and a plethora of visitors who wanted to see what went on at the infamous Government Center. It was clear that the Iraqi workers had told Eng. Mahmood that they would not go if they had to be part of such a large convoy. Eng. Mahmood insisted that there was no problem; they would just meet us at the repair. "You remember where break is, Lt. Legge, don't you?" said Eng. Mahmood in front of my superiors and everyone else in the lobby of the Government Center. This was getting a little embarrassing.

In the meantime, the commander of the convoy was calmly talking in my other ear saying that there was no way in hell they were going to let the workers just go as they pleased. The other units would shoot them down for certain, probably just to make a point.

Although it was not what I was thinking in my head, I said, "Not a problem at all. Eng. Mahmood, I know that your workers do not like the tanks, so it will just be Staff Sgt. Pool and me. You know Staff Sgt. Pool, don't you? He helped you with the checkpoint in your neighborhood a week or two ago."

Staff Sgt. Pool stood there with a blank look on his face and held his hand out to shake Eng. Mahmoods, only because he did not know what else to do. Eng. Mahmood stuck his hand out with the same look of confusion as Staff Sgt. Pool. I just kept talking. "This is no problem at all. So where are your workers right now?" "They are out front," replied Eng. Mahmood. Before he even had a chance to say another word, I interjected, "That is just fine, we will meet you out front and we can drive together. You can tell your workers that they will recognize us, and we will just follow them at a safe distance. This will be a great day for everyone." I was escorting Eng. Mahmood out of the lobby as Staff Sgt. Pool and all the other Marines just stood in silence.

As soon as Eng. Mahmood had left, the Staff Sgt. and his commander said at the same time, "What the hell are we doing?" Col. Burdine, my CO, was standing there and was curious as well. I said, "Let's ease up behind them with just two vehicles. Everyone else can just give us a little space, and as we get rolling, they can start closing the gap and get in regular convoy formation." Everyone knew that not only was this not proper procedure, but it was not safe for the first two vehicles. Staff Sgt. Pool was lucky enough to be in the front vehicle with me. I turned to him and said, "Nothing but a piece of cake. But we gotta eat it NOW!"

Luckily Col. Burdine was standing there and said something to the effect of, "There goes Lt. Legge again."

It was just enough to get us all scrambling to our vehicles. There was absolutely no time to brief all the men waiting in their vehicles. I jumped in the lead vehicle and let the Marines, who knew what they were doing when it came to convoys, do their thing. A few quick orders were barked out and we were rolling. The amount of chatter on the radio was comical. Our standard operating procedures were to not say anything on the radio unless you had to. Too much chatter and no one could hear a thing. Everyone was calling out something to the effect of, "Where the hell are we going?"

We were not supposed to go out to the front of the Government Center. The back route was much easier and designed for our vehicles to pass through. In order to get to the front road, curbs were jumped, one way streets were turned to the opposite direction, and larger vehicles were simply shit out of luck. The two lead humvees, with me in the first, somehow managed to get to where we thought the telecommunication vehicles were gathered. Sure enough, they were just pulling out because they Eng. Mahmood had no doubt told them that we were going on a Sunday drive with them. We caught them just as they thought they were making their getaway.

I am not sure what possessed me, but I stuck my head up against the front windshield so they could see my face and waved at them as if they were part of a tailgating party on our way to the big game. I will never forget the look on those telecommunication workers' faces as they saw my face pressed against the windshield of a humvee in downtown Ramadi. Most were simply laughing. They still tried to give us the slip by going the wrong way down another one-way street leading out of town. We were right along side of them but separated by concrete barriers and concertina wire. I kept waving and smiling. Staff Sgt. Pool simply said, "This is all fucked-up." But as we traveled a little further out of downtown, the workers seemed to get used to the fact that a crazy Lt. was following them and all our units began to close in together making what now looked like an organized convoy.

We radioed ahead to up-coming units and everything seemed to be on track again. We had one scare when several tanks that were there to protect us while going through their area of operation came rolling up and got much too close to the Iraqi vehicles than they ever wanted them to. As a matter of fact, they came too close to our vehicles as well. Those tanks can be very intimidating. I turned back out the window, spotted the frightened Iraqis and gestured that they had frightened me as well. I think we almost lost them at that point, but they stayed on course.

As the convoy progressed, it became more and more calm and organized. The larger vehicles did their very best to keep out of sight while still maintaining the security they had been ordered to provide. To everyone's delight, there was not a single incident the fifteen or so miles we had to travel that day.

CHAPTER EIGHTEEN

OCTOBER 2005
DUE WEST OF HABBANIYAH, IRAQ

When we reached the site of the repair, we had instructed all vehicles not to swarm around the Iraqi vehicles. They carefully and quietly set up their strategic defense of the area. I got out of my humvee to greet the workers and to make sure they felt at ease. I walked over and said, "As-sallaamu-alaykum," which at that time meant, "Wasn't that a bunch of fun?" The workers actually looked happy (or maybe just relieved) to see me. They quickly got out of their vehicles and started to work. You can say anything you want about the Iraqis or anyone in the Middle East, but when they get down to work, they get down to work. Especially in an area known to have snipers.

They had a hole dug in Route Michigan within minutes using a backhoe. At just the right depth, the backhoe withdrew its claw and two workers with shovels were in the hole before the claw was completely removed. They began digging and soon had uncovered the infamous fiber optic line. I was beginning to think we would be back in time for lunch. This was not only good because I was already hungry, but sitting in one place anywhere in Iraq for any length of time is not good for your health. We were in an asbestos trash dump. I was wondering what I would have- roast beef or macaroni and cheese.

Once the line was uncovered, another worker jumped in on cue, spliced and crimped various lines, exposing the fiber-optic line. The line itself is made of a very fine and pure glass. Information is passed along it via light waves that travel the length of the line. This form of communication is considered the best median for transmitting large and high-definition data. The only problem is, because it is glass, it can break easily, especially when car bombs and IEDs are going off all the time. With the lines uncovered, another worker jumped into the hole with a much more sophisticated piece of equipment. After hooking his machine to the lines, he shouted something in Arabic, jumped out of the hole, and yet another worker jumped in to start reconnecting the lines.

Fiber-Optic repair conducted along Route Michigan.

One of my Iraqi telecommunication workers
uncovering the damaged fiber-optic line.

This was fantastic. A little anticlimactic, but fantastic nonetheless. And they said it couldn't be done. Just as I was preparing my acceptance speech for my soon-to-be promotion, they had already filled in the hole and I distinctly heard Eng. Mahmood say, "200 meters," as he pointed farther to the east on Route Michigan. They began to put all their equipment in their vehicles and moved down the road, one vehicle at a time. All the Marines who had set up their perimeters and were just becoming familiar with their fields of fire were suddenly forced to gather their gear, get in their vehicles and follow the Iraqis who were now a hundred yards down the road.

The Marines quickly set up another defensive perimeter. The Army moved their tanks. The drone that was in the area circled around the sky just a little further to the east. Things adapted quickly. The Iraqis, in the meantime, were doing their coordinated dance. Digging, splicing, crimping and testing.

After their routine was complete, Eng. Mahmood simply stated, "Forty meters," pointing in the same direction we had just come from. Again, they packed their gear in an orderly fashion and just as our Marines were getting settled into their new position, we were moving again. Tanks rumbled from their positions as well. By this time, the Marines were beginning to grumble. Word was out that these workers did not know what the hell they were doing and this was another wasted mission.

Security we had on Route Michigan during the fiber-optic repair.

The Iraqis were unaffected by anything we were doing. They had their job and knew how to do it. They carefully measured out the third move and Eng. Mahmood himself marked the spot where the dig would begin. He looked at me and gave me a wry smile as if to say, "Wait till you see how good I am." They dug this hole just as quickly as they had the past two holes. The backhoe went to its predetermined depth, workers with shovels quickly relieved the backhoe, the line was uncovered and within inches of the center of the hole, there plain to see was a portion of the cable that had obviously been damaged.

I thought we were home free and ready to head back to the barn. This was not the case. It turned out that this was just the beginning of our day out on Route Michigan. The actual repair of such a fine and pure glass is not an easy thing to do. I was later to talk to an American expert in fiber optics and he told me that it was "a bitch" to repair fiber optic lines in the confines of a sterilized lab, let alone outdoors, and in the desert to boot. Any foreign matter, i.e., dust, that comes into contact with the glass as you repair it makes the line worthless. These workers were not trained in sterile lab rooms; they worked in the desert. But this meant taking their time and often having to redo the repair upon testing the many lines.

All of this time the telecommunication workers were using to repair the lines the locals were using to spread word that the infidels were in town. We had completely blocked off Route Michigan so that no vehicles could pass through. But there was a side road in the desert to the north where the occasional car or truck would amble by. If they lingered too long, trying to catch a glimpse of what we were doing, the tanks would roar their engines and chase them away like elephants brushing away bunny rabbits from their watering hole. Some vehicles would circle around for a second and even third look only to be chased off by an M1 tank at full speed.

One vehicle was just way too curious for our liking. It was a Datsun B-210 that kept circling around, trying to get a better look at what we were doing. It had been chased off several times but we could not seem to discourage its curiosity. Word went around that one of the tanks was going to "light him up." This meant that it would fire on the vehicle, but only to scare it a bit.

I went to all the workers to warn them that there was going to be gunfire but not to worry. It was only meant to scare off a vehicle that might endanger them. They were not happy to be in the middle of a firefight. Luckily, the Datsun saw we were about to do something about its presence and disappeared into the desert.

We were out there for a good five hours. All Marines and soldiers were in their armored vehicles the entire time except for Staff Sgt. Pool and me. I had to be out because they were my workers, and I had promised I would be with them the whole time, but Staff Sgt. Pool did not. The majority of the time, he was either watching out for me or going from vehicle to vehicle to be sure his men were doing their jobs and were all right.

We heard on the radio that sniper fire had been detected and were firing on us, but to tell you the truth, I never heard either the gunfire or rounds go by. Other than that, we made it through the whole day without a significant attack. The young Marines were a little disappointed but this old Marine was happy as a lark. Eng. Mahmood finally declared that the fiber-optic line was fixed, and we all packed up and left the desert near Habbiniyah.

The repair made international news. It was the first time the lines of communication were open all the way from the Syrian border to Baghdad. This was a very big deal for the Iraqis. Eng. Mahmood was considered a hero among the Iraqis, not just in Al Anbar Province, but in Baghdad as well. This was a huge coup for him.

I later found out that this line only serviced around 68,000 customers, but I guess they were really important customers. More importantly, and much less obvious, this got us working together. Many of us and many of them shared in a feeling of accomplishment that night. Some in Arabic. Some in English.

CHAPTER NINETEEN

OCTOBER 2005
RAMADI, IRAQ

After the success of getting the fiber-optic line up and running, and my developing relationships with the telecommunication workers, I was sent an e-mail saying that it would be incredible if we could get the Tips Line up and running as well. I responded to the e-mail saying, "Aye, aye, sir, will get right on it."

I thought my best plan of attack would be to find out what the heck a Tips Line was. I had heard the term mentioned a couple times and knew that it had been down for almost a year prior to our unit getting there, but I thought it was a line of people who had had too much to drink, therefore a bit tipsy, and were waiting on some sort of taxi.

Turns out I was wrong again. The Tips Line was a direct telephone line that any citizen in the town of Ramadi could use to make a call which would go directly to an interpreter in Camp Blue Diamond, where the phones were manned twenty-four hours a day. The call could be made anonymously and was used to report things like someone burying a roadside bomb along route Michigan. This was the number one problem for troops in our area of operation. On a small three-mile stretch of road, it was determined that we were losing a Marine a week more than we were when the Tips Line was operating.

After doing some research on repairs that had been attempted in the past, it appeared that there was some kind of break in the line under the traffic circle, directly in front of Hurricane Point. This was a notorious spot where firefights broke out on a regular basis. My first thought was, "Oh good, another friendly working atmosphere."

I am going to jump ahead just a bit and give away the ending. We were successful in getting the Tips Line up and I received an award for my part. It was the Navy and Marine Corps Achievement Medal (referred to as a "NAM"), and this is what it says:

"DEPARTMENT OF THE NAVY
THIS IS TO CERTIFY THAT
THE SECRETARY OF THE NAVY HAS AWARDED THE
NAVY AND MARINE CORPS ACHIEVEMENT MEDAL
TO
FIRST LIEUTENANT ERIC F. LEGGE, UNITED STATES MARINE CORPS RESERVE
FOR
FOR MERITORIOUS SERVICE WHILE SERVING AS THE GOVERNANCE TEAM LEADER FOR COMMUNICATIONS FOR DETACHMENT 1, GOVERNMENT SUPPORT/PROVINCIAL CIVIL MILITARY OPERATIONS CENTER, 6TH CIVIL AFFAIRS GROUP, 2ND MARINE DIVISION, FROM 1 TO 11 OCTOBER 2005. DURING THIS PERIOD, FIRST LIEUTENANT LEGGE QUICKLY ASSESSED A CRITICAL NEED TO REPAIR THE DIVISION'S TIPS LINE AND RAPIDLY DEVELOPED A PLAN WITH PROVINCIAL IRAQI GOVERNMENT OFFICIALS TO REPAIR IT. WORKING CLOSELY WITH DIVISION STAFF OFFICERS AND MARINES FROM 3RD BATTALION, 7TH MARINES, HE INFLUENCED AN IRAQI PHONE TECHNICIAN TO APPROACH THE WORK SITE THROUGH AN EXTREMELY DANGEROUS SECTION OF THE CITY OF AR RAMADI AND MAKE THE NECESSARY REPAIRS. OVERCOMING INSURMOUNTABLE CHALLENGES, SUCH AS INSURGENT OBSERVATION AND LANGUAGE DIFFERENCES, HE PERSONALLY ENABLED THE RECOVERY OF A CRITICAL COMMUNICATION ASSET THAT PROVIDES DAILY INTELLIGENCE FROM IRAQIS REPORTING INSURGENT ACTIVITY. FIRST LIEUTENANT LEGGE'S INITIATIVE, PERSEVERANCE, AND TOTAL DEDICATION TO DUTY REFLECTED CREDIT UPON HIMSELF AND WERE IN KEEPING WITH THE HIGHEST TRADITIONS OF THE MARINE CORPS AND THE UNITED STATES NAVAL SERVICE."

That is actually the first time that I have ever read the entire award. Pretty darn impressive if I say so myself. Wish I could just end the book here. It would kind-of be like getting a hole-in-one in golf, then just walking off the course and never playing again. That way, if anyone were to ask if you are a golfer, you could casually say, "Yep. Last hole I played, I had a hole-in-one." The fact that you shanked a shot into the trees, it bounced out of the trees and into the bunker where it hit a rake, then bounced into the air, hit a sprinkler head and bounced into the hole… no one need know about that. My award was not exactly a shank in the trees, but after receiving it, I sent an e-mail back to my family and said I was coming back with a heck of a story. I told them it was a long story that ended with me in my underwear in downtown Ramadi.

I think if you ask anyone who has ever received a medal for doing something in combat, they will tell you that it sounds a lot better on paper than the way it actually happened. In my case, a whole lot better. First let me say, I am very proud of my NAM. But, it is not exactly the highest award ever given. To say it is not exactly the Medal of Honor would be the understatement of all times. It is actually the lowest award you can get and still call it an award.

I received my NAM on the fifteenth day of December 2005, alongside one of my good buddies, Duane Fish, who was also receiving a NAM for pumping out the septic tank at the Government Center. I don't want to take anything away from Fish's NAM because it was a very dangerous job, but I will always look at my NAM and remember our shitters.

CWO 2 Fish after a long day in the flooded
court yard of the Government Center.

My award also alludes to the fact that I knew exactly what I was doing, did it quickly, and saved the day. Could not be further from the truth. As I said, I did not have a clue what the Tips Line was or how in the world I was going to do anything to get it repaired. I looked through all the correspondence from the past year about attempts to get it up and running, and everyone seemed to come to the same conclusion. It was damaged beyond repair and situated in a place that was simply too dangerous to work. Not that our communication guys had not tried; it was simply a lost cause. I just love lost causes.

I went to Eng. Mahmood and asked him if he knew anything about it. Because we were now brothers who were destined to die together, as he had put it several times in the past, he told me he knew about the problem with the lines. I could sense it was a subject he was not interested in talking about. It did not take me long to figure out there were those who did not want us to succeed in Iraq, and especially did not want the local citizens helping us by reporting their nefarious activities. Eng. Mahmood even discussing this with me could not only put his life in danger, but also his entire family.

I did not press the issue with Eng. Mahmood that day, but I continued to talk to our Marines on the ground who were in charge of communications. The more I learned, the more determined I was to get this Tips Line up again. One of the translators who helped man the phone when it was working said that the Tips Line not only helped soldiers and Marines, but had also saved the lives of hundreds of local Iraqis. It helped in ridding the streets of roadside bombs, which did not discriminate between civilian, soldier, man, woman or child. I had heard too many stories of kids playing along the road and stumbling onto an IED. This Tips Line was something everyone except the insurgents would benefit from.

After a couple more missions where I accompanied the Iraqi telecommunication workers, making certain they were not only protected by the coalition troops but also were not fired on, the workers and I could not help but create a bond. Even the hardcore haters of anyone in uniform could not help but laugh at my incredibly broken attempts in trying to speak their language.

On the long days of watching two men dig a hole while six or seven of us stood by and watched (certain people simply could not be seen with a shovel in their hands), I would casually bring up the Tips Line. I began to get more and more information about what was wrong with it and who knew how to fix it. It was just my luck that the person who knew most about the line was Hamad, Eng. Mahmood's first cousin.

One thing I admire most about the Muslim faith, yet also have the most reserve about, is their intense loyalty towards those they befriend. It need not be someone they have known for a long time or one from their religion. If you somehow become part of their lives, they are obligated to protect you. It makes no difference what your religion is; they feel obligated by their religion to protect you. Just read the book, "The Lone Survivor," by Naval Seal Marcus Luttrell. He was caught in a very bad situation in a small Afghanistan village and the local Muslims took him in at risk of having their entire village wiped out by the Taliban.

I decided to use this dedication to their religion to get the Tips Line repaired. I pressured Eng. Mahmood to have Hamad meet me at the Government Center for a meeting. He eventually succumbed and set up the meeting. Hamad showed up out of respect for his cousin which gave me the chance to ask him what it would take to repair the line.

Eng. Mahmood was in the meeting but we had no interpreter. Eng. Mahmood knew enough English and I had learned enough Arabic to make the meeting work. I asked Hamad if it was possible to have the Tips Line repaired. Even I could understand his reply. Eng. Mahmood made the translation anyway. "Very easy," was all he said. I asked the question several different ways because it just seemed too simple for them to say it could be fixed easily. They replied time after time, "Very easy."

I was told that all Hamad had to do was be given access to the hole under the traffic circle and he could have it repaired in no time. I was very skeptical but after the meeting, sent an e-mail to all concerned, including my command, that we could in fact fix the Tips Line.

The reply I got was absolutely comical. It was sent from a LtCol in the communications section and went something like this:

"Although I appreciate this young Lieutenant's enthusiasm, we have reviewed this situation thoroughly and it is not as simple as the young Lieutenant makes it out to be. We will not, however, get in the way of his attempt. Any resources from our unit needed will be provided."

It was clear that the LtCol had never met me, but to this day, I appreciate him calling me the "young Lieutenant." It was the only time I was ever called "young" during my entire tour. I was given contact information for a real "young Lieutenant" so I gave him a call. He was hesitant to give me too much support because we had never worked together. He also had firsthand experience in trying to get the Tips Line up, only to end up being fired on. He questioned me about the Iraqi who was assisting in the repair and was more than hesitant in trusting him. I assured him that I trusted him and said that I would be there for the repair.

Eventually the 1st Lt agreed to try and set something up but insisted that it be done in the cover of darkness. Preferably at 2:00 or 3:00 in the morning. Marines own the night.

I went back to Eng. Mahmood and Hamad the next day and tried to make arrangements to do the repair at night. This idea was flatly rejected. Eng Mahmood did not like the idea of working at night and from the look on Hamads' face, there was no way he was going along with the idea. They objected even further to working with the Marine Corps unit in the area. Hamad said over and over, "I fix myself, OK?" I had a feeling this would not go over well with the unit in charge of the area. I was right.

There was absolutely no way they were going to allow an Iraqi to climb into a hole right in front of an important outpost without supervision. I tried to convince my command to let him do it, but they also said that if anything were to happen, it would not be good.

I went back to Eng. Mahmood and Hamad to plead my case, but the resistance had grown since our last meeting. At this time in my tour, I had never pulled the Muslim guilt card. I thought it was time.

I became angry and came close to insulting the two of them, saying that I thought we would "die together," as Eng. Mahmood had said several times in the past. I also ensured Hamad that I would be there every second to be sure absolutely nothing happened to him. After only a few comments taking this approach, Eng. Mahmood said that they would do it. He meant that Hamad would do it. Hamad had a horrified look on his face but had to go along with his cousin's decision.

I went back to my command and said that "my" Iraqi worker would do the repair, but that it had to be done during daylight hours. After sharp resistance to the idea, I used the same tactic with my own Marines. I said that I was going on the repair and if they did not want to accompany us, we would do it alone. You simply cannot shame a Marine. They reluctantly set a date and a time for the beginning of the next week.

The hesitant nature of this unit doing the mission had absolutely nothing to do with cowardice on their part. They were only concerned with the men whom they would have to charge with completing the mission. I, on the other hand, only had my own life on the line. Those who made the decision to go forward with the mission had by far the more difficult decision. They had the lives of the Marines they were in charge of on the line.

So, we were set. A week from the next Monday, at 0800 in the morning, we were to meet at the small base just across the street from Hurricane Point, called the JCC. I had nine days to make all arrangements. I have no idea what JCC stands for but it was a place where Iraqi vehicles are held once impounded for one reason or another. It was not uncommon for Iraqis to go there demanding their cars back. Hamad was never going to go into Hurricane Point, which was purely a Marine Corps base. I tried to have the meeting set for 10:00 in the morning, a much more reasonable time to have an Iraqi worker show up, but was quickly turned down by the Marine Corps unit involved.

Again, I set a meeting with Eng. Mahmood and Hamad, both of whom were growing tired of a project much more dangerous for them than me, and I told Hamad when we were to meet. When announcing 0800 in the morning, he immediately gave me the blank stare that I had anticipated, meaning he would show up when he felt ready. I told him that I would arrange a convoy of five vehicles to take him from the Government Center to the JCC, only some two and a half miles away. It would be a very quick ride that would only take three or four minutes tops (when we went down route Michigan, we hauled ass). Hamad did not just say no, but he said hell no, in a form of Arabic that is saved for showing great disdain.

I argued with Hamad for at least an hour. I pulled out the shame card again but soon realized that he was not going to budge on this one. He was never going to get in one of our vehicles and that was that. I told him that we would just follow his vehicle but he wanted nothing to do with that either. We finally decided that he would drive a garbage truck to the JCC, and I would be there in advance. It was not how we wanted the mission to go, but it was the best idea I could come up with. Everyone bought in on the plan, and the wheels of a mission slowly began to turn.

It sounds simple. Just wander down to the JCC around 0700, wait on old Hamad to show up, walk across the street to the hole that was only 40 yards away, hook up a couple of wires, then take the rest of the day off. But nothing in Iraq was simple and nine days was pushing it for everyone involved. There were at least five units needing to be briefed about exactly what we were going to do. The unit protecting Hurricane Point, which was stationed at the JCC, my command, air units protecting the area, and two other units in the area needed to know what we were doing so that no one saw us as a threat. Bad things happen when some Lance Corporal sees something in his field of fire that he had not been briefed on.

Everything actually went much more smoothly than I had anticipated. All units went along with the plan according to what was needed to accomplish the mission. All I had to do was get to Camp Blue Diamond two days prior to have time to get prepared with the other unit, then go to the JCC the night before to greet Hamad when he arrived in his garbage truck the following morning. It was only two and a half miles. Certainly a Marine could make that distance with no problem, right?

There were no issues making the initial arrangements to get there. A convoy was coming to the Government Center two days before the mission to drop off a couple attorneys who were involved in paying claims to Iraqis whose property we had inadvertently damaged. I would jump in the empty seat, return to Camp Blue Diamond, and then jump on the convoy that was making a supply run to the JCC the following day. It was only an 800-yard trip across the bridge over the Euphrates to the JCC.

Could not be easier, right? Any true athlete or competitor knows that is the worst thing you can say.

The day before the mission was to take place, all hell broke loose. A couple of Marines were killed and all convoys were canceled. I worked all that day, trying to make arrangements to get to Camp Blue Diamond, the JCC, Hurricane Point, Camp Ramadi, or anywhere west of where I was. Nothing went that day.

Not a problem. I still had a day to get there and be ready for the mission. But again, there were no convoys going anywhere the next day either. By 1600 Sunday afternoon, I was in a panic. I was not going to let this mission fail. It would have taken weeks to get it back together and I could not bear the idea of having a mission fail over a lousy two and a half miles.

I went to our Commanding Officer, Col. Miles Burdine, at the Government Center with an alternative plan. I told Col. Burdine that I was going to jump in the back of the garbage truck that Hamad was driving to the JCC. I knew that Hamad would slow down enough to let me jump on. All I had to do was convince Col. Burdine to break every rule in the book to let me go unaccompanied with an Iraqi civilian driving down the most bombed street in Iraq.

I was very persuasive and Col. Burdine actually considered the plan of simply turning his back while I jumped in the truck. But, soon after my crazy presentation, he refused to let me go. I don't blame him. If anything were to happen to me, he would have had paperwork to fill out for the remainder of his tour. The truth of the matter was, he could not make a decision that he knew was going to endanger one of his Marines. This was a decision that all commanders have to make every day. I know for a fact that I could not make such a decision.

I was still not ready to give up. I was so set on getting this mission accomplished that I was thinking about climbing over the wall late at night and just walking the two and a half miles. But, the highest Commander intervened.

At 2200 that night, out of the blue, a convoy showed up at the Government Center. I ran across the courtyard to see where they were going and if they could drop me off at the JCC. The SSgt. in charge of the convoy thought I was crazy and said he was not going to the JCC. He also did not have any open seats in the convoy.

I am not sure if Col. Burdine spoke to the SSgt. himself, but for some reason, the SSgt. came to me and said that he would find me a seat but that he would only take me to Hurricane Point. This was right across the street from the JCC so I gladly accepted his conditions.

He went to the last up-armored humvee, opened the back door, ordered a Lance Corporal out of the humvee and to jump in the back of what we called a bucket truck. A bucket truck is nothing but a humvee that has an open back end, similar to a pickup truck. It is designed to haul around supplies that don't die when they get shot. There is a very short sheet of paper-thin metal in the back that is designed to keep whatever you are hauling from falling out. It is not designed to protect troops.

I was standing by the door as the SSgt. was shouting at the Lance Corporal out of the humvee. I saw the terrified look in his eyes as he immediately did what the SSgt. said. As he was getting out of the humvee, I put my hand on the SSgts' shoulder and told him that I would ride in the back of the bucket truck. The Lance Corporal did not say a word. The SSgt. looked at my single bar on my uniform and said, "No sir, he will go back there." The young Marine would have done exactly what he was told, but I was not about to make that nineteen-year-old get in the back of a bucket truck just because my mission was falling apart.

The SSgt. was pissed that he had to deal with me in the first place and just said, "Whatever you say, sir."

So, I climbed in the back of the bucket truck. I have no idea who that Lance Corporal was, but if you are reading this book, you owe me a beer. We sat in the parking lot at the Government Center for fifteen minutes, I felt safe there because after all, this was my home. The ride to Hurricane Point was only two and a half miles away so the ride could only be four, maybe five minutes tops. I thought, what could happen in five minutes?

I just love to challenge old Murphy.

CHAPTER TWENTY

OCTOBER 2005
RAMADI, IRAQ

You would think that a two-and-a-half mile trip in vehicles that have no speed limit would be a quick one. Well I am here to tell you that it was the longest trip I have ever taken and I have driven all across this country. As previously stated, one thing I have really tried to do in this book is to simply state facts, not opinions or over-dramatize anything.

So I met up with this convoy at 2200 (10:00 at night for you civilians), we sat in the parking lot for fifteen minutes before we finally got on the road. We started down route Michigan just as we had done fifty times before, petal to the metal and hauling ass. I was sitting on a spare tire in the back of the bucket truck, hunched over with my head between my legs, just as we are instructed to do when we have no armor protecting us. This provides the smallest silhouette for someone to aim at. I braced myself for the hopefully four minute ride. But as soon as we seemed to get up to the usual speed, we came to a screeching stop. What the hell were they doing?

We were now just two blocks from the Government Center in the absolute worst part of downtown Ramadi. Like a good Marine, I kept my head down. I was certain there was some kind of mechanical problem with one of the vehicles ahead of us, and this was only a temporary pause. We would be back up to speed in no time. Remember, speed is our friend. I did not time this stop but my estimate is that we were there for at least five minutes. I sat with my head between my knees and did not look up once. The roar of the engine sounded and we were off again! What a relief!

Then, just as before, as soon as we got to what I thought was a comfortable speed, we came to a screeching stop again. By now I simply had to know what was going on. I would rather have been shot than not know why the hell these guys were stopping in the middle of route Michigan. So I uncoiled from my brave bent-over position only to see that we were now stopped right under the Rasheed Hotel. The Rasheed Hotel was a five-story hotel in the middle of Ramadi, only four or five blocks from the Government Center, where snipers were daily taking pot shots at the Government Center. We had recently hit it with a five hundred pound bomb, dropped from a F-18, hoping to deter anyone from climbing back up the battered five stories to shoot at us again. This only seemed to stir up the ant pile.

So here I was, sitting directly below the Rasheed Hotel in the back of an open truck! My first instinct was to change sides in the back of the truck. I moved to the other side so at least a little of the paper thin metal would cover my ass. I looked up again and saw the building on the other side of the street from the Rasheed Hotel. Hadn't I read some kind of report that said snipers who had been shooting at us from the Rasheed had moved to the other side of the street? I quickly moved back to the other side. No, wait a minute, I had read some other report that stated they had easier access to the Rasheed and were still shooting at us from there. I quickly changed back. Maybe they had gotten their hands on our report and decided to switch to the other building just to keep one step ahead of us. I jumped to the other side.

By this time, I was laughing so loud at what must have looked to all those Iraqi eyes I could feel watching me in the dark of night like a Marine who was completely insane. After what seemed like an eternity but in reality only a few minutes, we started off again. I continued to laugh uncontrollably. I stuck my head between my legs again, fully realizing that I was sporting at least a half-moon to all of Ramadi with my butt sticking up in the air. To this day I am willing to swear that the only reason I did not get shot sitting in the back of that bucket truck under the Rasheed Hotel is because the sniper stationed there was laughing as much as I was and simply could not get his sites to stop moving. I even think I heard the laughing.

Three or four blocks from the Rasheed, we stopped again. By this time I could care less about my safety. That ship had long since sailed. I now stood up in the back of the truck to see just what the hell was going on. We were right in front of one of our small outposts called Snake Pit. Two seven-ton trucks pulled into the small parking lot in front of Snake Pit where I saw a couple Iraqis with their hands bound behind their backs, being escorted into one of the seven-tons. Holy shit, I got myself on a detainee convoy!

One of the disadvantages of being at the Government Center was that once you were there, you were stuck. Coming and going from the Government Center was simply too dangerous, so all convoys in and out were only done when absolutely necessary. We were allowed to go on a quick convoy to Camp

Blue Diamond every other week to get some hot chow and decent showers, but for the most part, we really did not get to see the sites of Ramadi. That night, I got to see all the sites. What was supposed to be a five-minute convoy ended up being just over an hour and forty-five minutes through the city of Ramadi. We finally got to Hurricane Point just after midnight. My sides were hurting so bad from laughing that I had a hard time sleeping on the marble floor just outside the control room door, awaiting my last leg of the trip.

I slept there because although I was no more than seventy yards away from the JCC, I still needed to grab another convoy to get me right across the street. The Marines at Hurricane Point were not at all happy to see me. Why on earth did they have to organize five up-armored humvees, along with at least twenty Marines, to take some incredibly old first Lieutenant seventy-five yards across the street? I told one of the Sergeants in the command center to at least warn the sentries at the front gate not to shoot this old Lieutenant as I ran across the street, because I was going to get across that street.

He must have said something to his people because by 0700, they had arranged a convoy to take the pain-in-the-ass Lt. across the street. It only took me seven hours to go that last seventy-five yards. I was getting things done now. By 0703, I was where I needed to be- at the JCC.

The JCC is a small building across from the traffic circle in Ramadi where Thrift and I had our famous collecting of barbed wire by way of Humvee rear axle. None of us really knew what its' primary mission was, but it had something to do with coordinating with the local Iraqis when their vehicles were impounded or they needed to get an ambulance. There were several interpreters who lived at the JCC, so it was not considered by the locals as being a coalition forces building.

By 0730, the communication guys from 3/7 had arrived and all that was left to do was wait for Hamad. 0800 came and went and my fellow Marines were already becoming antsy. They were not as accustomed to the timing habits of the average Iraqi as I had become.

0900 also rolled by with no sign of Hamad. The grumbling became a bit louder.

1000 came even slower than the previous two hours, probably because I was holding my breath, and still no Hamad. By this point, the 1st Lt. in charge of the communication Marines was not at all a happy camper.

"I think it is time to call this a no-go," was the only thing this young 1st Lt. would say for the next hour. By 1100, Marines were beginning to pack their gear to get the hell out of Dodge. I remained as optimistic as I possibly could, but my assurances of Hamad showing up were wearing thin. I had also run out of, "If he is not here at the top of the hour, we will pack it in," since two top-of-the-hours were already gone. For the next forty-five minutes, I did everything I could to convince these Marines that this mission was not only important but that I was positive it would be a success. They were all getting very tired of listening to me, but gave me one more top-of-the-hour. Then, regardless, they were out of there.

At 1145, a cab pulled up to the front of the JCC. We all went outside to see what was going on, and reluctantly, out came Hamad. In hindsight, I am glad I did not jump in the back of a garbage truck passing by the Government Center the night before. Hamad did not look happy to be there at all. In spite of his loose-fitting clothes (customary clothing in the Middle East), you could visibly see Hamads' entire body trembling. He looked at the approaching Marines in uniform, armed for battle, and you could see him move back towards the cab to make a hasty retreat. He glanced at the still-open door, then back towards the approaching Marines. Luckily, he spotted me amongst the Marines and immediately sighed. You could see the relief on his face. I raised my hand to wave hello.

I moved toward Hamad and shook his hand. His hands were shaking almost uncontrollably. I greeted him with the formal "As-sallamu-alaykum," which means "Allah be with you," and he quietly mumbled "Wa-alaykum-assalam," meaning "May Allah be with you." I then said "Kayfa-Ha-Lak," which means, "How are you?" and all I got in response was a blank stare. I did not need a translator to tell me that Hamad wanted to say he was anything but fine and there was a good chance he would never be fine again.

I signaled Hamad to go towards the JCC building so that we could get ready for the repair, just yards away. Hamad froze in fear and refused to move. We were out in the open driveway of the JCC building and although there was some protection from the sandbagged walls that had been constructed to prevent suicide vehicle car bombs from entering the facility, it still felt like we were in the open. Hamad refused to go in the building. He reminded me of a dog that was simply not getting into the bathtub.

There was a small-bunkered guard shed out in front of the JCC used as a vehicle checkpoint for the Marines on the outer perimeter of the building, so we all tried to seek shelter in this little shack. Although I did speak a little bit of Arabic, I quickly sensed we were going to need someone who spoke Hamads' language. An interpreter was sent for as I tried to get Hamad to stop trembling.

When the interpreter arrived, Hamad immediately told him that he did not need all these armed Marines and would "go fix hole." The interpreter explained to me that Hamad wanted to walk across the street, do the necessary repairs by himself and be on his way. To be seen with all these Marines meant certain death for him once word spread that he had helped us. The 1st Lt. of 3/7 said in no uncertain terms Hamad could not go alone because it was

Marine property, therefore it required to have Marines present if anyone was going to touch it. We went back and forth on this issue for the next thirty minutes and neither side was budging. Both Hamad and Marines were simply ready to call it a day rather than give in to the other side.

I instructed some of the Marines who could not fit into the small shack to "cover our perimeter," which meant finding somewhere else to stand while I tried to convince Hamad to work with us. I told him we would simply put him in the back of a bucket truck, which would be completely safe (me laughing on the inside, recalling the previous night), then surround the truck with our other vehicles and back the truck up to the hole. Hamad and I would jump in the hole and he could make his repairs. I assured him I would be there every second.

In the meantime, the 1st Lt. was questioning whether the repair could be done at all. He asked Hamad the same question I had asked the previous week. "Are you sure these lines can be repaired?" Hamad kept saying in Arabic, "You take the blue wire, connect it to the yellow wire, ground it to the black wire and all fixed." The 1st Lt., at one point, turned to me and said something along the lines of, "I'll bet he can memorize the Los Angeles phone book as well." I sided with Hamad and told the 1st Lt. that Hamad had never let me down before. The 1st Lt. threw up his arms in disgust and said, "Whatever," but insisted he was not letting Hamad go alone.

It was time for me to work on Hamad. I assured Hamad that I would not let anything happen to him, but he said it was not being in the hole where he worried about getting killed; it was once someone recognized him and word got out that he had helped us. I told him he could wear my helmet and shirt so no one would recognize him. I quickly took off both my helmet and shirt and handed them to Hamad before he had time to think about it. He reluctantly put them on, but the trembling did not subside.

He again said that he would be recognized. He said someone would see his eyes. I quickly got my goggles and sunglasses out, and Hamad put them on. He said that someone would recognize his sandals, so off came my boots. During this gradual strip tease, the 3/7 1st Lt. was becoming more and more uncomfortable. I assured him that I would be fine; I just needed a helmet to meet the necessary requirement to be "outside the wire," along with my flak jacket. When Hamad finally said that someone would recognize his pants, without hesitation, I said, "No problem," and began to take off my pants. I can't recall who protested more that I was soon to be in my underwear in downtown Ramadi- Hamad and the Iraqi interpreter or the Marines, but I did not get my pants halfway down before everyone shouted, "No," all in unison and plain English.

I did not shout nor direct my statement to anyone in general, but I explained very firmly that we were going to get this repair done, in my underwear or not. One of the extra interpreters in the background watching the spectacle at the time ran back into the JCC building to bring back a generic uniform the interpreters wore. Hamad returned what I had given him and slowly put on the new uniform. I put my uniform back on and tried to convince Hamad that everything would be fine. But his trembling continued. Once Hamad had completely covered himself from head to toe with something from either the interpreters or me, but he still refused to go with us. He again begged to just let him walk across the street and do the repair by himself.

I turned to the 3/7 1st Lt. and by the look on his face, I did not need a response from him. No escort, no repair. It was time to put my knowledge of the Muslim religion to work.

"Your cousin, Eng. Mahmood, gave me his word that you would help us, and you told me last week that you would help. Are you a man of your word or are you going to shame your cousin?" I said this, knowing it would strike a nerve, which I admired in the Muslim religion but also knew full well was at the heart of why we were being attacked day in and day out. The fact that his cousin was a man well respected amongst the citizens of Ramadi also carried a lot of weight.

Hamad did not say a thing. "Your cousin said that he and I would die together because Allah willed it when we were not all killed outside of Habbiniyah. You were with us in Habbiniyah, weren't you?" Hamad said nothing. I knew that I was getting to him so I thought I could at least sweeten the pot. "I will give you twenty dollars of my own money if you do what you have said you were going to do." Believe it or not, twenty dollars to a common worker is not a small amount of money, but the amount really meant nothing. The fact that I, a friend of his and his cousin, was asking him a personal favor made it to where he could not refuse unless he wanted to disgrace his family.

After almost an hour of working on Hamads' emotions, his pride, his religion and even his anger, he agreed to get in the back of the truck. I turned to the 3/7 1st Lt. and said, "We don't have much time." I wish I could remember that 1st Lt.'s name because I have never seen any Marine get a mission together as fast as he did. Within minutes, Hamad and I were in the back of a bucket truck, surrounded by five up-armored humvees and were on our way across the forty yards to the hole were the repair was to take place.

We had to block off traffic going through the traffic circle, but we decided to let one lane pass through so that there would not be a traffic pile-up and curious bystanders sitting around watching our repair. We backed the truck right over the hole and Hamad and I jumped in. To be honest, it was a little anti-climactic. I was picturing a deep, dark cave or tunnel, going under the street with danger hidden in the darkness. Truth is, it was just a dang hole alongside the road that Hamad and I barely fit in. He immediately went to work, uncovering wires that had clearly been blown apart by some kind of roadside bomb. I tried to be of assistance but was just getting in the way.

I eventually jumped out of the small hole to give Hamad some room to work. I stood there at the traffic circle in downtown Ramadi. All the other Marines were either in humvees or strategically placed behind walls, rocks, or light poles, guarding the mission should we get into a firefight. M-16s, 50-cal machine guns, all locked and loaded, ready for anything. In the meantime, there were vehicles driving by, straining to get a peek at what we were doing. A large population of pedestrians walking from miles away to conduct business as usual in the war-torn city also tried to get a peek at what we were doing.

Because I was not part of their unit, I was not about to ask what the hell they wanted me to do in assisting protection of the mission, and I am absolutely certain they did not want me to help guard the perimeter, so I just sat out there in the middle of the traffic circle and did what I did best. I waved to all the Iraqis passing by, yelling out, "Marhaba." This was the informal way of saying hello. I figured that due the current circumstances, we were all family anyways.

I was surprised to see that I recognized at least one out of every ten Iraqis walking by. An attorney who came to the Government Center practically every day who I tried to help out as much as possible walked by, so I yelled out, "Marhaba." He was a kind, older gentleman who really appreciated all that my fellow Marines and I tried to do for the citizens of Ramadi. We had actually become friends. He even gave me a bottle of cologne for Christmas as a gesture of friendship (and to continue receiving preferential treatment, I'm sure). At first, I wanted to tell him we could not accept any kind of presents from them, but I could tell in his eyes he really meant it as a gift from one human being to another, so I accepted and thanked him.

He was not expecting to see me among the heavily armed Marines at the traffic circle, so when he recognized me, he quickly smiled and began to raise his arm to wave from across the street. He just as quickly realized where he was, surrounded by his fellow Ramadians, and pulled his arm back to his side, averting his eyes so no one knew we were acquainted. It hurt me a bit, but I understood the position he was in. It was the same position Hamad was in. He and his family could be killed that night should anyone think they were assisting the infidels.

I stood out there waving and shouting "Marhaba" to everyone who walked by. Some laughed, some spit on the ground to show their disrespect, but most just knew we were doing our job. The hatred was only about ten percent of those who passed by that day. I have felt the same amount of hatred in several major cities in our own country, and in those, I was not in uniform.

I wish I could have stood out there longer because it was an uncommon opportunity for us to be imbedded in the locals' part of town with so little protection and armament, but Hamad was done in twenty minutes. He jumped out of the hole and said, "All fixed." We Marines just looked at each other, many not as happy about being with the locals as I was, so Hamad and I jumped into the back of the truck, and the other Marines got into their humvees and we left. We had no way of immediately testing our work because communications with the other end, at Camp Blue Diamond where the Tips Line came out, had gone down.

We dropped Hamad off in front of the JCC where he quickly took off our infidel clothing and disappeared into the crowd. The 3/7 Marines took me to Camp Blue Diamond to find out if we had accomplished anything. We located the Marines who we had lost communication with. They were standing out in no-shade, 120-degree weather, wondering where the hell we had gone. I don't know enough about communications to know how they could tell, but after attaching some gadget to the wires of the Tips Line all I heard was, "We are up again."

This is the first time I have told that whole story. When typing, "We are up again," tears came to my eyes. Not just for the success of the mission, but what was soon to follow.

CHAPTER TWENTY ONE

OCTOBER 2005
CAMP BLUE DIAMOND, RAMADI, IRAQ

It turned out that there were seven Tips Lines that went into various departments in Camp Blue Diamond, and Hamad had managed to get five of them up and running. The mission was considered an overwhelming success. My command was so thrilled, they gave me permission to stay at Blue Diamond for a couple nights to get some rest until the next convoy came, and then I would go back to the Government Center. I was thrilled but exhausted. I planned to get some sleep, but before I did, I went to the five locations where the Tips Line was back up and listened to the beautiful sound of a dial tone.

I have never slept as soundly as I did that night. Before or since. The adrenaline was wearing off and I slept like a baby. The next day I went to the chow hall to get some hot food and could not help but smile all day. Many of the missions I had previously been on really had no immediate results. This was immediate. If nothing else went right in my tour, which was more than likely, this feeling of success could not be taken away. At least not until the next day.

After having noon chow, I went to our command office at Blue Diamond where they were more than happy with the results. I also went to the 3/7 communication command office and thanked them for all they had done in getting this mission accomplished. They had done far more than I had in preparing logistics, and I just had to meet the Lt. Col who in a previous e-mail had called me the "young Lieutenant." He never said anything about my age when I introduced myself and told him how outstanding his men had been during the repair, especially the other "young Lt." who had acted so quickly and efficiently, but I could tell he was shocked at my age.

I had evening chow and again fell fast asleep. I was woken early the next morning, and told I had a call from my unit at the Government Center. I was told that I was to go to our command center and call them as soon as possible. I quickly got dressed and made the ¾-mile walk to 6th CAGS headquarters. I was expecting to hear that they too were thrilled about the mission's success. When I got to 6th CAG headquarters, I was greeted not with smiles but concerned looks and was told to make my call.

I did not think too much about the looks, just thought they were busy with the next order of business. I went to the phone and called the Government Center.

"This is Lt. Legge and I was told to check in," I said to the lance corporal who answered the phone.

"Yes sir, Lt Col Glover needs to talk to you."

It was a little unusual for Lt Col Glover to want to talk to me directly, but I was certain it was because he needed me to send him a report on the mission. He was always on my ass to get my reports in on time and hated the fact that I could only type with two fingers. He was a hard core Marine who never once gave me a single break. I completely respected the man and years later, when he retired at the Pentagon, he asked if I could fly from Dallas to DC to be there at the ceremony. I told him I would not miss it for the world.

Lt Col. Glover got on the phone and in his usual Marine Corps, no-nonsense way, informed me that they had learned Eng. Mahmoods' cousin had been killed the night before. He wanted me to hear it from him and not through the grapevine. I guess everyone at headquarters already knew of the news because I simply hung up the phone and left the office. I began to walk back to my trailer and the CAG XO followed behind me. Our XO for the CAG was an outstanding female Marine, Lt. Col. Pratt. I never could beat her time in the three-mile run. It kind of pissed me off, but I had such respect for her.

I think she called out "Lt. Legge" several times as I was walking in a daze back to my quarters, but I honestly did not hear her. She finally grabbed me by the shoulder from behind and asked if I was OK. I told her I was fine and again began walking. She stopped me again and asked, "Lt. Legge, are you alright?"

LtCol Pratt, the Executive Officer of 6th CAG.

I turned again and said, "I am fine, ma'am. Better than fine because I found out how good I am at my job. Hamad said he would get killed if he helped me, but I did not let that get in the way of the mission. I did everything I was trained to do and more. I knew how to get him in that hole and I did. I am damn good at my job." By this time, the tears could not be held back. I have always been good at getting people to do what I want them to do. I have a gift of bullshit that can make someone feel good about doing something they do not want to do at all. In this case, I got a man killed. But the mission was a success. That's all that mattered, right?

Lt Col. Pratt could tell that I needed to be alone. She told me to get some rest, and then go see the Chaplain on base. I went back to my trailer and fell asleep again. When I woke, I did what I was ordered and went to see the Chaplain. He was a nice fellow, Navy guy, volunteer, and was used to listening. I told him that I was ordered to come see him and he asked, "What for?"

"I got a man killed the other day."

"You mean you lost one of your Marines?" was his reply.

"No, I got an Iraqi killed on a mission."

"Well, Lt., that is your job. Killing is never easy, but it is your duty to follow orders," the chaplain said.

I then explained what had happened, and that it was bothering me that because I had been so persuasive, a man had lost his life. I don't think the chaplain had come across a confession like that before. He even admitted he was a bit perplexed, but he assured me that in the eyes of God, I had done nothing wrong. I know he meant well and was doing his job, but when I left, I only felt worse.

For the next three days, I was in a fog. I managed to write a letter to Hamads' wife, which I showed to my command to get authority to send. This is the letter I wrote:

"To the family of Hamad:

My name is 1st Lieutenant Eric Legge. I am the Marine who was with Hamad the day he helped us fix what we call our Tips Line. It is a direct line to our Division Headquarters where the citizens of Ramadi can call in anonymously to report any activity in their neighborhoods that may cause the deaths of our soldiers or the citizens of Ramadi, such as planting of explosive devices. The Tips Line has not been working for many months and the amount of bombs that have been planted along the roadsides in Ramadi has grown significantly. Thanks to Hamad, many lives will be saved. Not just the soldiers' lives, but innocent men, women and children of Ramadi. Hamad is a true hero amongst those who want Iraq to be the country that it will eventually become. A country where it is safe for the children of Iraq to play, without fear of losing their lives, as Hamad did.

I personally wanted to tell you that I will never forget his heroic act. I cannot begin to tell you the sorrow I feel for my part in Hamads' death. He knew how dangerous it was to help us. I convinced him that everything would be all right. We did everything we could to conceal his identity. I even took my uniform off and gave it to him so that no one would recognize his clothing. Unfortunately, my boots were too small for him, as they will be for the rest of my life. Although he was covered from head to toe, I could see in his eyes he felt our disguise would not save him. He was right.

There is nothing I can do or say that could possibly express both my sorrow for my part in Hamads' death or the honor I feel for having met such a heroic man. I would like you to have something that means a lot to me. This gold pocket watch is a possession that means more to me than any other possession I own. It is not the most valuable as far as what it is worth, but the possession I would least like to have lost. My oldest child was to get this when I die. She knows how much it has meant to me and has always told me that it is all she ever wants should something happen to me. I know that she also would want you to have this because of the lives that Hamad has saved. Someday I plan on bringing her, my three other children, and the grandchild that is on its way, to Iraq and show them the beautiful country that Hamad helped to build.

Forever in your debt,

1st Lieutenant Eric F. Legge, USMCR"

When I returned to the Government Center, I had piles and piles of work to be done. Everyone and their cousin in the city of Ramadi seemed to want something from me, but the only person I wanted to see was Eng. Mahmood to give him the letter for his cousin's wife, along with the gold antique pocket watch. For some reason, I took it with me to Iraq. It was one of my most prized possessions. Not that it was worth all that much; I had far more valuable possessions, but it was something of mine that meant the most to me. It was true what I wrote to Hamads' wife. I hadn't asked my daughter if it was OK to give to someone else, but I felt that it belonged to Hamads' wife and believed my daughter would agree.

The gold watch I was to give to Hamad's wife.

I tried everything to get in touch with Eng. Mahmood. I was usually successful in tracking him down, even if the phone lines were down. But this time he was nowhere to be found. I assumed he was at some type of ceremony for his cousin's burial. I had given a lot of thought to my attending the services, but came to the conclusion that my presence would not help

Hamads' family. It would most likely create a disaster, so I put that idea out of my head.

Two days later, Eng. Mahmood showed up at the Government Center, saw me and gave me his usual big smile, and said, "Lt. Legge. You have been gone too long." I did not know what to say other than, "I am so sorry about Hamad." He looked at me as though I knew something he did not. I again repeated my sorrow for Hamads' death and that I felt responsible. Eng. Mahmood again looked at me perplexed.

"Hamad not dead, Lt. Legge. He not dead."

"I don't understand," was all I could say. "Hamad not dead at all," he repeated. "I was told your cousin had been killed," I said, not letting it sink in that Hamad was still alive.

"No, no. That my cousin in Habbiniyah. He very old anyway."

"So Hamad is alright?" "Yes, Lt. Legge, he very good. He happy you give him money but you not need to do that," said Eng. Mahmood, apparently embarrassed that I had paid his cousin. Hamad would have done it just on Eng. Mahmood's word alone.

A wave of relief came over me. I could feel the emptiness inside slowly filling back up with life. The numbness also began to go away as well. It did not happen right away, but after a day or two, I felt like I was back to normal. At least as normal as you can feel in a battle zone.

To bring this story to an end, just a couple of days later, Hamad was going to do a repair on the telephone lines in a war torn part of Ramadi. I had given him one of my letters of deconfliction and had worked things out with the unit that was very close to where the repair was being done. Only problem was that units of tanks were passing through the area as Hamad was getting out of his vehicle. One tank stopped and the turret gunner took aim at Hamad. Hamad saw this but had no fear because he had a letter signed by Lt. Legge saying it was OK to dig here.

Hamad started toward the tank, holding my letter over his head and saying, "Lt. Legge, Lt Legge." The turret gunner had no idea what a Lt. Legge was, saw Hamad approaching his tank as a threat, and opened fire on him with a fifty-caliber machine gun.

I am not going to leave you hanging, thinking poor Hamad was really dead this time. I am certain that absolutely nothing will ever kill Hamad. He will live to be a hundred and ten years old. He will, however, have two scars on both cheeks of his face where one of the fifty-caliber rounds passed through, not even touching a single tooth in his mouth.

For anyone who knows anything about weapons, especially the fifty-caliber machine gun, this sounds like a fish story. But sure as hell, three days later, Hamad showed up at the Government Center- first to show me the holes in his cheeks, but more importantly to put in a claim for some American money he heard they were giving out for such unfortunate accidents. Hamad simply could not contain himself when he saw me.

"Lt. Legge, Lt. Legge! You must see!" exclaimed Hamad in muffled English due to his injury. To be honest, I had absolutely no desire whatsoever to see his wounds, but knew there was nothing that was going to stop him from showing them to me. He carefully removed both bandages, and sure enough... holes in both cheeks. Hamad must have turned and screamed as that gunner fired on him with his mouth wide open. Allah took care of the rest.

We quickly processed his claim and gave him $2,500 on the spot. Hamad had had a very good week. $2,540 would feed his family for at least two years.

CHAPTER TWENTY TWO

DECEMBER 2005
RAMADI, IRAQ

Things just seemed as though they could not go better. We were working together and things were getting done. We immediately jumped into the next repair that Engineer Mahmood had been asking about for weeks. It was not far from the Government Center, just east on route Michigan in front of one of our more dangerous outposts called Camp Corrigador.

Camp Corrigador was just on the outskirts of downtown Ramadi. It was one of the more rough outposts because it did not have the best of "housing" for the troops there. The troops peed in pipes that had been buried into the ground at an angle and the rest had to be done in bags and burned on a regular basis. Surrounding the camp were residents who often challenged the Marines stationed there at night. Roadside bombs were common and EOD had their phone number on speed dial.

A roadside bomb had gone off in front of Camp Corrigador several weeks earlier, taking with it a buried telephone line that serviced one or two neighborhoods in the area. The residents had been pressuring Engineer Mahmood to have it fixed as he had done for other neighborhoods. Engineer Mahmood and I decided to take advantage of the momentum we had in both his workers and the coalition forces in the area to get this particular repair done.

The repair itself did not present nearly as many obstacles as the other repairs we had recently done. It was just down the street and the units involved were those I worked with daily. The only concern was being out on that stretch of street, which was dangerous in spite of the fact it was directly below a two-manned over watch armed with a fifty-caliber machine gun. The Iraqi workers were the ones who were most concerned. They had a strange aversion to our fifty-cals. I assured them there would be no problems and I would be there to be certain they were safe.

Two days prior to the scheduled repair, I was informed there was another agricultural conference in Baghdad that I was to attend. I would have to leave at the same time the repair was to begin. I could not go on the repair. The Iraqi telecommunication workers were a little concerned that I would not be there but I told them that Staff Sgt. Pool, who had been with us at the fiber optic repair, would be there to keep them safe. They remembered the Staff Sgt. and that he too had been walking around with us as we repaired the fiber optic line. They agreed this would be fine.

The day of the repair came and everything was going more smoothly than any mission we had prepared to date. The Iraqi workers were not only on time, but they agreed to meet at the Government Center and take the short trip to the repair with our Marine convoy. The Marine unit was there on time and hooked up with an Army unit that was going on the repair as well. I met with the workers who were going on the repair to send them off with a smile because Eng. Mahmood was not going on the trip either. They were happy to see me but had been under the impression I was going with them. I again explained my situation and that Staff Sgt Pool would be there along with Major Johnstone, as I had told them two days prior. They again recalled Major Johnstone and Staff Sgt Pool and agreed to do the repair. All were ready to get another successful repair done. The Iraqi workers and my fellow Marines left the Government Center together. This was a historic moment.

I heard the massive explosion at the Government Center as I was packing for my trip to Baghdad. At the time, I really did not think much of it. We had become immune to explosions around the Government Center because they went off so frequently. Several minutes went by as I continued packing when the commotion began. We were on alert all the time since we were attacked virtually every day, but this was not the commotion of a "regular" attack. Something was definitely wrong.

I went to the communication center within the walls of the Government Center and could immediately tell by the tone in everyone's voice that this was not an insignificant explosion. Their voices seemed to have a higher pitch and their speech a little more rushed than the typical calm of day in and day out. It quickly dawned on me that this explosion involved the convoy that I should have been on. I stood out of the way, trying to piece together what had just happened, straining my ears to hear any kind of radio transmissions. It was clear there were casualties because they were clearing the way to the nearest medical facility. The local hospital was nearby but we did not have it secured. It was strictly for the local Iraqis. The decision was made that they would haul ass to Camp Ramadi, four miles away where they were already preparing for emergency treatment.

One transmission I did catch was the sound of Major Johnstone giving an assessment of the situation and that medical assistance would be needed immediately. I also heard that someone had been strapped to the hood of the humvee. Although I was relieved to hear Major Johnstones' voice, I could not help but wonder who was strapped to the humvee. I was praying it was not Staff Sgt. Pool. I also did not want it to be one of "my" Iraqi workers, but the thought of losing one of the Marines in my unit was not something I was ready to accept.

Several long and agonizing minutes went by with no word about the injured. The Marines in the communication center for 3/7 in the Government Center kept asking if "any of ours" were among the injured or killed. Finally we were informed that all coalition forces were fine but two Iraqi workers were badly injured, though still alive and conscious. This was a relief to me beyond any words I can find.

Twenty or so minutes later, as the two Iraqi workers had been taken to Camp Ramadi and were placed in incredibly capable hands, I heard from Major Johnstone. All he could tell me was that he was getting out of his vehicle, had just turned towards the Iraqi vehicles and the bomb went off. He was thrown to the ground, as well as Staff Sgt. Pool who was closer to the blast. From that point on, all hell broke loose. The Iraqi vehicles, along with the Army contingency in the convoy, simply took off. The only remaining were two Iraqi workers lying on the ground.

There was not enough room in the remaining humvees, so they strapped the victims onto the hood of the humvees. This was actually common practice for our own wounded Marines. They raced them to Camp Ramadi where they were quickly taken care of. The first question that I just had to ask was, "Are you guys alright?" Major Johnstone said that he was fine and although Staff Sgt. Pool had taken some shrapnel, he was fine as well. When I asked how the Iraqi workers were, all he could tell me was they had suffered mainly lower body injuries and one of the workers knees looked as though "someone had taken an ice cream scooper and taken two chunks out of his knee caps." I latter saw pictures of my Iraqi workers' knees and he could not have described it any better.

Staff Sgt. Pool received the Purple Heart for the injuries he sustained in the blast. I don't know what medal, if any, Major Johnstone received for his action, but as far as I am concerned, he deserved at least the Bronze Star. The actions he and his men displayed during that chaotic moment embody the integrity that makes Marines so proud to be Marines. Their mission was to protect those workers, and at the risk of their own lives, they did exactly what they were supposed to do. When we all came back to the states, and some family members were at Camp Lejeune, I ran into Major Johnstones' wife and young daughter. Although I am sure his daughter did not care what I said about her dad and was simply happy he was home, I just had to tell her that she should be very proud of her daddy. He had done one of the most heroic things that happened during our entire tour.

CHAPTER TWENTY THREE

DECEMBER 2005
RAMADI, IRAQ

Although the mission had taken a horrible turn, at least no one had been killed. That is what I had been told. Minutes later, I received a call from Eng. Mahmood. His voice was higher pitched and faster than usual, sounding just like the Marines in the 3/7 communication center. He asked me if we had his injured workers. I assured them they were in good care and had been taken to Camp Ramadi, which had some of the best medical personnel in the world. I told him that from what I had been told, both men were in stable condition. I would update him as soon as I heard anything.

Eng. Mahmood was clearly disturbed and slightly confused. He asked again if anyone had been killed and I assured him that they were badly injured but both were conscious. He asked something about one having an "injured foot." I told him that I did not know the extent of the injuries, but yes, both had suffered injuries to the lower body. I said I had been told that one suffered injuries to both knees (thinking that this is what he was after), but all he could say was "No, foot." Again, I told him I would keep him updated on their injuries.

Thirty minutes later, Eng. Mahmood called again. This time he was in more of a panic. He again asked me, "Is there worker that injure foot?" I again said they both had injuries to their legs, but he became more insistent- "No, foot. We find shoe in truck," exclaimed a now out-of-control Eng. Mahmood. I asked him to repeat what he had just said and he repeated, "We find shoe in back of truck." After several attempts to try and put together what he was trying to tell me, I told him I would call the hospital and find out about the injuries.

I hung up and found the number to the hospital in Camp Ramadi. After explaining who I was and what information I needed, I finally got hold of one of the medical team who had worked on the two Iraqis, and explained that Eng. Mahmood kept asking me if one had a foot injury. I was told they had received shrapnel to the majority of their lower extremities, but their feet were not damaged that badly. I then asked, "Was one of them missing a shoe?" The medical worker seemed irritated that I would ask such a stupid question and said he did not think so.

I called Eng. Mahmood, and relayed what I had been told. I said that they thought both had their shoes on when they arrived. I suggested that maybe one of the workers had removed his shoe after the explosion and left it in the truck. This time Eng. Mahmood said, "No, no, not shoe! Foot!" I did not know what to say. "What?" was all that came out. Eng. Mahmood was now speaking in more Arabic than English and my Arabic was not very sharp. I quickly called for one of the interpreters. Bill, a great interpreter who had been with us for quite a while and had a very good relationship with Eng. Mahmood, got on the phone.

After several minutes of talking to Eng. Mahmood in Arabic, I became impatient and insisted Bill tell me what was going on. He put his hand over the receiver and told me that one of Eng. Mahmoods' workers was missing and had a hurt foot. I asked him how they knew his foot was injured. Bill asked Eng. Mahmood and then turned to me and said, "They found his foot." I shook my head and asked, "Did they find his foot or did they just find a bloody shoe?"

Bill went back to the phone again and talked with Eng. Mahmood for several minutes until he noticed I was again becoming impatient. He placed his hand over the receiver and explained to me that the workers in the truck had taken off after the explosion and driven home. When they got home, they looked in the back of the truck and saw a shoe. They picked it up and saw the foot was still in it.

There is not much you can say to something like that; take it from me. I was certain the two workers who had been taken to Camp Ramadi had not lost feet, so there had to be another missing worker. I asked Eng. Mahmood to tell me how many workers were missing. He said three. We needed to find another body.

I called the unit at Camp Corrigidor that was involved in cleaning up the mess and found they had gone out to one of the vehicles on fire to put it out, and had received gunfire. They tried a second time and again where fired upon, so they just left the vehicle out there. I asked if they had seen another body and they said no. They assured me that they would go out the next day and do further investigations.

I called Eng. Mahmood again and told him they had not found a body at the scene but had been run off by gunfire. By this time I could tell he was exhausted so I told him I would call the next day as soon as I heard anything. He reluctantly said, "Ok" and hung up the phone. The next day, before I could call him, Eng. Mahmood called me. "They find body?" was all he said. I told him I would call the unit again. Eng. Mahmood said that the worker's wife was in an absolute panic and we must find his body.

It is very important to the Muslim faith to bury their dead quickly. I understood that Eng. Mahmood was in charge of these men working for him and to at least retrieve the body was extremely important to him. I called the unit again and it was still too hot of an area to go into. Eng. Mahmood called at least three times a day for the next three days with only one thing to say. "You find body?"

We never did find the body of that worker. A thorough search was done of the area, mostly due to my persistence in badgering the unit in charge. They went out into a very hot area receiving enormous resistance from insurgents, but no body turned up. The neighbors in the area were all questioned but nothing was found through their interrogations.

I tried to get the telecommunication workers out again to make that repair and others, but the momentum was now at a standstill. We never recovered from that incident for the rest of my tour.

CHAPTER TWENTY FOUR

OCTOBER 2005 thru MARCH 2006
THE GOVERNMENT CENTER, RAMDI, IRAQ

Life in battle is not all serious and foreboding. The fact of the matter is that the majority of the time, we soldiers of war look for things to get us into trouble. The amount of practical jokes and just plain old idiotic behavior increases with the degree of danger you are surrounded by.

The Government Center courtyard was sometimes used as a temporary morgue where the bodies of killed combatants were stored in body bags until the proper units could come do their jobs. One of the 3/7 Marines thought it would be a hoot to play a practical joke on one of the very young Marines. He climbed into an empty body bag and thought he would give the private a bit of a scare.

It was a miracle that the young private did not unload his full magazine that he had locked and loaded in his M-16 into the corporal that slowly unzipped the body bag as the innocent private walked by. But such is war. You really need a distraction from the chaos that often goes on around you. That is what started the 22:00 Club.

I truly regret to include this in this book because if anyone does actually read this book, I run the risk of having the "videos" reach the public where they were never intended to go. One video in particular floated through the halls of the Pentagon shortly after we were sent home and I barely lived through that ordeal. The idea of some of the things we did in the 22:00 Club being told out loud sends shivers down my spine. But the fact that several were recorded for history on video, and can be replayed for anyone to see, is mortifying.

Let me explain the 22:00 Club. As I have stated, the 3/7 Marines was the

Marine unit that was there to protect us CAG Marines at the Government Center. They were on the rooftops and occupied the sparse second floor of the building that was adjacent to ours. On that second floor was their Command and Operation Center (COC) where they had a TV monitor, which fed in the video of the camera that was placed in our lobby by the front entrance.

Because of our rules of engagement as CAG Marines (do not fire even if fired upon if at all possible) they wanted to at least have a camera in what was considered to be our most vulnerable spot. If shit hit the fan there, we were in some really deep shit. But it was incredibly important for our mission not to have "combatants" actually stationed in our building or the locals would not feel as free to come and complain to us.

So up there in the COC of the second floor, some poor Marine had to sit and stare at that stupid monitor to be certain we were not under attack. I am not sure what possessed me, but I thought it was our duty as CAG Marines to somehow thank those 3/7 Marines for keeping such a watchful eye on us. Thus gave birth to the 22:00 club.

One day deep into our tour, I thought I would at least bring a little entertainment to this desolate part of downtown Ramadi. I went up to the COC and told the young Marine who was watching the monitor that a female reporter from CNN was in our building and that she had the terrible habit of taking a sponge bath in the head we reserved for visitors and female Marines that from time to time visited the Government Center. I then explained to the now extremely interested Marine that she would then walk down the hallway at exactly 22:00 (which was covered by the camera) in nothing but a skimpy towel. I warned the young Marine to simply avert his eyes at 22:00 so as to not over excite him.

As I walked away from the COC, I knew that my bait had been taken. Sure enough, by 21:45 that evening, that small COC room, no bigger than a small bathroom, had every 3/7 Marine not standing a post squeezed into every available inch that had a view of the monitor.

This is where things turn ugly. Needless to say, we had no female reporter in our building, but we had the next best thing. Fish. I know I have mentioned Chief Warrant Officer Duane Fish before. What I have not mentioned is that Fish was at least 6'6" and had one of the hairiest backs I personally have ever seen. Wrapped in a small white towel and a mop on his head, from behind he was the spitting image of Marilyn Monroe.

At precisely 22:00 that evening, Fish, in all his glory, simply strolled by the camera and down the hallway out of view of the twenty or so 3/7 Marines whom we could hear bursting into laughter 300 yards away. The first of many performances of the 22:00 Club was now in the books.

CWO 2 Fish in the debut performance of the 22:00 Club.

The co-conspirator, and the real brains behind the 22:00 Club, was Major Juliette Chelkowski, our Public Affairs Officer (PAO). Major Chelkowski had done some acting in Los Angeles and simply had an artistic eye and a flair for the dramatic.

Major Chelkowski among a happy group of girls in school.

What started out as fifteen second skits, such as an unnamed Marine walking hand in hand with one of the male interpreters (a common thing among men in the Middle East) quickly by the camera, escalated to elaborate productions involving props, extras, lighting, and a key grip. I never did figure out what a key grip was.

One of the more elaborate skits we performed was our version of "West Side Story." Major Chelkowski was the director and around five or six of us were the performers. I really do not remember anything about the plot of this two or three minute skit we enacted in front of the camera which fed our stellar performance live to the awaiting 3/7 Marines, nor do I recall what was latter to be named at the Pentagon "the twinkle toe move," but videos seldom lie.

Major Chelkowski gave us a quick briefing of what she expected out of us, we did a practice or two to get our blocking and positioning in order, and we went live. There was some confrontation among rival gangs (as in the actual "West Side Story"), there was some strolling around eyeing each other, fingers snapping to the imaginary music, trying to look both cool and tough at the same time, when it happened. I don't remember doing it, I don't remember what I was thinking of at the time, and I am still sure someone placed it in digitally, but for some reason I did a little flutter step with my feet as if I were a little ballerina.

When I got a call from one of my fellow Marines stationed at the Pentagon a couple of months after we had arrived to the safety of the good old USA, I had no idea that I would soon wish I was back at the Government Center being shot at. He explained that there was a video being sent around that he was certain I would want to see. I asked what it was and he said this was something that had to be seen, not described.

When I opened up the video he sent via e-mail and pressed play, I immediately recognized the stark surroundings of the Government Center. I felt at home again. As the video played on, I also recognized the characters slowly coming into view of the hand held video phone that did not produce the highest quality of videos. But there I was. There could be no denying. The video played on and I was a little embarrassed that this skit of our 22:00 Club had somehow made it to the Pentagon, but I did not see anything that would warrant it being sent to me. I did not see "it" on the first viewing.

I called the number that was on my fellow Marines e-mail and said, "I don't know what the big deal is."

"You didn't see it did you?" he replied.

"See what?"

"I didn't see it at first either" he said. "Let me send you a more enhanced version," he said with a slight chuckle.

A minute or so later I had another e-mail waiting in my inbox. I opened, pressed play and the same video played again as it had a few minutes earlier. This time, something did catch my eye. As the video was coming to a close I was about to rewind and play it again, but the Marines who had viewed it in the Pentagon were kind enough to automatically have the video play again.

This time as the video played, they had somehow put a shadow highlight that directed the viewer's eyes to one of the characters feet. Needless to say, they were my feet. As I strolled around my adversaries in the script, snapping my fingers and looking cool, for some unknown reason I did the flutter kick. It being highlighted in the video made it impossible to miss. The fact that the Marines who had highlighted my feet also thought it would be nice to reverse and replay the flutter kick over and over again exaggerated the action that might have otherwise gone unnoticed by mankind.

There were many more skits we performed as the 22:00 Club. Those of us brave enough to be at the hands of our confident director were sometimes filmed, sometimes not. The 3/7 Marines got such a kick out of it they actually did a performance for us. I think I was in Baghdad at the time because I first saw the video not long ago when I was visiting Major Chelkowski and her husband whom she had met at the Government Center while he had a short tour of duty with the State Department. I was amazed at the ingenuity and talent that these war hardened Marines showed in their version of the 22:00 club.

I was at Major Chelkowski's wedding a year ago in San Antonio where the groom's cake was a replication of the Government Center where they had met. Keith told the wedding party how they had met in Ramadi and what stood out most about Major Chelkowski was how good she smelled. I just had to ask him if I had smelled better would I be standing up there instead of her?

Major Chelkowski received the Combat Action Ribbon for her duties performed at the Government Center. This is a distinction that not many Marines receive, let alone female Marines. I was lucky enough to be involved in a mission she was in charge of setting up a foot patrol that was going to pick up some computers left in a building that was too dangerous for even the local Iraqis to go to. Of course when we got there, the computers were destroyed, but we had a great time getting there.

CHAPTER TWENTY FIVE

JANUARY 2006
AL ANBAR PROVINCE, IRAQ

I tried for weeks to get the telecommunication workers back out to do repairs that would benefit their communities, but the atmosphere after the bombing was one of, "It will not happen to me." I even tried to persuade them to work by telling them if they did not come with us, we were going to make the repair ourselves. Nothing worked. All of the work we had accomplished in the past months meant nothing.

To those who hated our progress- the insurgents- they were frightened of the progress we had made. Not only were coalition forces actually working with Iraqis, but communications that were once nonexistent, keeping the Iraqis in the dark (which is exactly were our opponents wanted them to be), were now up and running. The Iraqis from one area were talking to those in other areas and the word being passed around was that these infidels were not as bad as everyone kept telling them. They evidently decided this kind of talk had to stop.

On or about January 3, 2006, six of the major telecommunication buildings in Al Anbar Province were either bombed or torched, rendering all communications in Al Anbar Province nonexistent. Not a single phone worked anywhere. No one could talk to anyone. This is exactly what people who do not tell the truth want from those whom they are trying to control.

It was hard enough around the Government Center to get meetings organized when we had communications up and running among the local Iraqis. Now we could not get anything organized. Things came to a grinding halt. But the lack of having meetings was just the tip of the iceberg.

Communications is the key to civilized society. With no phone lines, ambulances that would ordinarily let our units know they had an emergency were now too frightened to make their runs. Police whom we had helped organize in the city were also staying in their precincts rather than making critical patrols. Everyone in Al Anbar Province virtually stayed in their homes.

This was unacceptable to the coalition forces because Al Anbar Province had become the poster child for what could happen in Iraq. Going into our tour, Al Anbar Province was considered a lost cause and we were only supposed to keep it from getting any worse. The thought of it improving was not even in the equation when we arrived. But things had been turning around. The December 2005 election was a 2,751% increase from the elections just eleven months earlier; a 60% turnout of those who were eligible to vote. I think this is one of the "statistics" I was most proud of while over there. The other accomplishments had a huge impact for Al Anbar, but I could not even begin to put them into quantitative measures.

The insurgents had done their homework. They knew just what buildings to hit to have everything go down. The bombing and torching were equally successful. I was immediately told to drop everything and to make an assessment of the damage, cost of repairs and how long it would take to get communications back up and running. I was also tasked with coming up with an immediate "band-aid" to get at least some kind of communications going. My first thought was to get a bunch of string and cans. This did not receive a single laugh. Marines don't like strings and cans.

I wanted to arrange a meeting with Eng. Mahmood but had no way of getting in touch with him. I had to rely on the old-fashioned Iraqi way-through the grapevine. It is amazing how quickly word of mouth spreads over there. When we wanted to clear out Fallujah in early 2004, all we had to do was tell the Mayor of Fallujah that we cared for he and his family, and if he cared for his family as well, it would best for them not to be around the following Tuesday. Within two days, the entire city of Fallujah- over a hundred thousand people simply vanished.

I told one of the Iraqis who worked at the Government Center that I desperately needed to talk to Eng. Mahmood. The next day, there he was. He had already been to three of the six buildings to do his own assessment and had sent others to the remaining buildings for damage updates. He was pissed. Eng. Mahmood, and really all Iraqis with whom I had come into contact, have more than just pride in their work. It becomes a part of them. For someone to destroy his work was like killing part of his family. He explained to me in detail the damage to all six buildings.

Most of Iraq's telephone lines were the old-fashioned copper lines. Cooper melts easily and whoever had done this knew that. The lines and the switches were melted beyond repair. It would take brand new switches to get things back up and running. Switches were not just expensive but hard to come by. Eng. Mahmood did have a bit of good news. He assured me that we would not need to have six new switches. He could combine some of the areas together with new technology. He also told me he wanted to go with what is called local wireless loop technology. I completely agreed with him even though I had not a clue what he was talking about.

After our meeting, my command wanted a complete briefing and plan of action. Col. Burdine said he had to get on a helicopter that evening for Baghdad to brief the really high-up chain of command. I gave him a quick rundown of the meeting and what needed to be done. He told me to prepare a PowerPoint presentation explaining what had been hit, where it was, what exactly was affected and how soon things could be back up. Oh, and he was nice enough to give me two hours to have it done. I told him it was no problem if he could just get my secretaries from Dallas to me in the next ten minutes.

My typing abilities were famous among my command. I was constantly asked why, if God gave me ten fingers, I only used one. I did the best I could in getting as much detail in the presentation as possible with the limited time I had. Fifteen minutes before Col. Burdine was scheduled to leave, he looked at what I had drawn up and just said, "Legge, you're going too. Pack your gear." For those who have never been asked to do something by a Colonel or above, there is no back-and-forth discussions, especially when you are a 1st Lt. I ran to my quarters and threw together what I thought I would need for the trip. Five minutes later I was standing at the door to the courtyard, ready to jump in a vehicle to take the convoy to the helicopter pad.

We went to Camp Blue Diamond to meet with Col. Brier, the commanding officer of our entire unit. At 0300 that following morning, we were off to Baghdad. As I have stated, Baghdad was not my favorite place. It was nothing but politics to me. It seemed as though there was a lot of wasted time spent there. I preferred being in the trenches where there was much less talk. But we must have our politicians and committees, whether we like it or not.

I managed to get a couple of hours of sleep, but we were scheduled for a briefing at 1030 that morning and the two Colonels wanted to meet an hour before the meeting to go over what we had. We met in the embassy building's lounge, which was a big open space with tables and chairs dispersed throughout. Coffee and donuts were on every table with four or five people at each, discussing the important things on their agendas for the day. Our table was no different.

"Well Legge, what have you come up with?" asked Col. Brier.

"Sir, as I have explained, they did a great job of crippling the communications in Al Anbar. There is no quick and easy fix. An estimate of getting back to the way it was is at least six months. There are alternative methods of communication that can be put into place, such as local wireless loop which is actually more reliable and faster to set up," I said with confidence. I had cheated a bit. I was at the lounge earlier, looking on their computers to find out what the heck local wireless loop communications were all about.

Turned out, this was a common type of communication system used in third world countries, especially those with desert climates. It utilized line-of-sight technology from one satellite dish to another. This eliminated the need for burying a bunch of cables and also eliminated roadside bombs from rupturing those lines. The dishes themselves were vulnerable but easily replaced. We could quickly get things back up in Ramadi using this technology. It was purchasing and having the equipment transported that I had no idea how long the bureaucracy and red tape could be pushed along.

We discussed the various things that needed to take place in order to get things rolling. One of the first questions that Col Brier had was whether Eng Mahmood was going along with this idea. Col Brier had a very clear idea on accomplishing our mission. It absolutely had to be not just with the cooperation of the Iraqis we were working with, but had to be their idea in the first place. It was a philosophy that made everything I had accomplished up until this time possible. I told him that it was Eng Mahmood's idea, and that he was pushing for it. He had even picked out what type of equipment he wanted and whom he wanted to buy it from. He liked Lucent Technologies because it was "much better." I had no idea this would later become a source of contention.

The next item we needed to discuss was what we were going to do immediately to get things back up and running. If we decided that day to go forward with the wireless loop, it would be weeks before the cogs of government began turning to get it in place. What could we do now to get things at least moving in the right direction?

I guess I reverted back to my childhood days when my sister and I played "Germans" on the grounds of my Grandfather's 120 year old church in Montclair, New Jersey, but all I could think of were walkie talkies. I just hoped we could find some that were a little better than the ones my sister and I had used. You could just yell at each other and it worked better than the walkie-talkies we had.

I presented the idea to the two Colonels, and of course they asked if I had come up with an alternate plan. I was ready for this line of questioning and was ready with an alternate plan. It was based on the wireless loop technology, but was based on smaller, portable units that could be put in place rather quickly. I had already looked on the Internet with rough estimates of costs and had asked Eng Mahmood what he thought about the idea. We discussed what it would cost and both came to the conclusion that to just get the city of Ramadi up with a very basic system would cost at least a half a million dollars. Beyond that, I knew that these portable units would also have to be guarded by our troops or they would not last a day. That would be a logistical nightmare that would never go through.

After briefing the Colonels of the pros and cons of each idea, all were in agreement that we would present the portable wireless loop idea first and once it became clear that more forces would be needed to protect them, everyone involved would start to lean away from the idea. Getting more troops was a very sensitive subject over there. Then we would bring up the alternate idea of walkie-talkies. I had also done some quick research on purchasing walkie-talkies in Iraq and was amazed to find out that they ran around $5,000 a piece for the encrypted type. Encrypted simply meant that the signals they put out could not be tracked by simple electronic listening devices and made the conversations between two sets a little more secretive. As one of the more knowledgeable communication guys I spoke with put it, "If I were talking on a non-encrypted walkie talkie, I sure would have one eye pointed to the sky looking for the laser guided missile that was about to blow my ass up because someone picked up on my signal!"

It was time for us to head to the meeting, so we were not able to come up with an exact amount as to our estimate of how many walkie-talkies we would need and what the overall cost would be. I was told to just do my best in the upcoming meeting and answer any questions I was given to the best of my ability. We picked up our gear and headed to the briefing.

CHAPTER TWENTY SIX

JANUARY 2006
US EMBASSY, THE GREEN ZONE, BAGHDAD, IRAQ

I was surprised at how many people were in on the briefing and even more surprised at their ranks. The average Marine could go through at least the first eight years of his career and only see two Generals up close and personal, let alone brief them. I had this beat by at least three. There were also many in uniforms, but no ranks on their collars. I had come to know what this meant. They weren't really there. I got a big kick out of those guys. We were all seated at the table and I was glad to see that Governor Ma'Moun was in on the meeting. I wanted to see what he had to say about what had happened.

The Governor was given the first chance to speak. I really did grow to admire Governor Ma'Moun, but when he got the floor, he was going to speak. It is nice to know that politicians, as well as people in general, are all the same, no matter where in the world you are. The Governor rambled for twenty of thirty minutes saying how this was a terrible act of violence against those in Al Anbar Province and that the guilty parties that carried out this dastardly dead needed to be brought to justice. I am pretty sure that what the Governor had in mind as far as justice was much quicker and more finite than we Americans are used to, and everyone in the room was aware of it. He also went on extensively about how important it was to get these lines of communications back up and running (he had just been given a computer with internet access and had a few websites he was missing).

After the customary length of time a man of that stature was expected to speak, he asked the senior most General in the meeting what he intended to do to fix the problem. The General quickly turned to Col Brier because it was his area of operation that was being affected. Col Brier assured Gov

Ma'Moun that we were diligently working on the problem and would have things up and running as quickly as humanly possible. He then turned to me, introduced me as the oldest 1st Lt in the Corps (I was beginning to hate that) and the meeting was then mine. By this time, nothing made me nervous, so I began my briefing.

I started with what damage had been done, where we had been hit, and the extent of how it affected communications throughout Al Anbar Province. I noticed that several in the meeting were both shocked and surprised to learn how bad things really were. I gave a brief explanation of what we planned to do for the long haul, explaining that it would take months to accomplish, and then began to talk about what we could do immediately. It seemed that most were much more interested in what could be done now rather than three months in the future. Most of those in the room knew they would be back home with their families by then.

I began with the portable local wireless loop idea, but as soon as I mentioned more troops would be necessary to protect them, just as we had anticipated, the room began to rumble. More troops were kind of like telling someone they needed to pay more taxes. Their eyes begin to roll and you completely lose their attention. A couple of the Generals asked my opinion about how many troops would be needed, and I gave them my best guesstimate. We quickly moved on to plan B.

I brought up the idea of the walkie-talkies as a very quick and temporary band-aid to the problem. I explained that the radius of effectiveness of this plan would be limited to five miles at best, but this would at least keep key buildings in communications with each other, such as the police stations, hospitals, and other much-needed support in the communities that had, until then, been taken for granted.

By this time, it was clearly about lunchtime because the hungry Generals were quickly losing interest in what the Old Lt had to say. It was announced that we would take a quick lunch break and at 1330, there would be a more precise plan discussed. We all left the room and Col Burdine took me aside and said, "You better have more details by 1330 or you are walking back to Ramadi." It was just a little before noon and I only had an hour and a half to have the details that these Generals were looking for. At least I thought I had an hour and a half until both Colonels I was with told me to meet them in the hallway by 1315 to brief them as to what I was going to brief the Generals. I should have seen that one coming.

As everyone was heading to the chow hall, I excused myself and darted down the nearest stairwell. I really had no idea where I was heading, but I knew there had to be answers out there somewhere. I had come to learn that in the Green Zone in Baghdad, you would be surprised what you could stumble across. You could even get a massage, if you asked the right people…which I did not for those with inquiring minds.

Once outside the embassy, my first instinct was to go up to the many MP's that surrounded the embassy. I had noticed that each had walkie-talkies themselves and maybe they could steer me in the right direction. I asked the nearest MP where he got his walkie-talkie and the blank stare was all I needed to realize that he was a waste of time. Just down the road was a police car that was parked with one of the MP's standing alongside it. I went up to him and asked, "Where do you guys get your walkie talkies?" He looked at me, thought I was kidding, but then looked me over again. You could tell by the wear and tear on a soldier's uniform whether he had come from outside the wire. I was also fully armed.

"We are issued our walkie talkies from the Motorola plant down the road a mile or two," said the dumfounded MP. When he said a mile or two, my heart sank a bit. I did not have time to walk two miles and back to get information from the Motorola plant. Plant? It made it sound like they were manufacturing walkie-talkies right there in Baghdad. I quickly explained my predicament to the two MP's who were now interested in what was happening outside the walls of the green zone. When they found that I had come from the Government Center, I suddenly had two friends.

"Do you know how I can get in touch with them?" I asked.

"We can do better than that. Get in."

I am certain that these two MP's were not authorized to act as a taxi service for transient Marines, but I could have cared less at the time. We drove what was at least a good two miles through the maze of roads that were within the walls of the Green Zone. I would never have found my way there myself, and we passed through all sorts of security gates that these MP's could easily get through. We finally came to what was known as the "Motorola plant." It was one of the warehouses that supplied Sadam Hussein's many palaces in the area. In these warehouses were all sorts of civilian contractors that supplied everything from walkie talkies to hand creams to keep you moist in the desert climate.

The MP's showed me to the Motorola plant and told me they would wait to take me back. I thanked them and went into the section that housed Motorola. It was nothing but your ordinary warehouse, with Motorola posters scattered along the barren walls. There were three technicians in the office area of the warehouse and as soon as they saw me, all three wanted to come see what the cat had just drug in. They did not say anything at first. They were too busy looking me up and down trying to figure out what the hell I was doing there. Finally, the tallest of the three, and probably the manager, asked, "What can I do for you?"

I explained my predicament as quickly as I could to them, and asked for ideas on getting communications into Al Anbar Province, and in particular, Ramadi. Now you have to realize, the contractors that do go into a battle zone are not only qualified technically in what they do, but are also proud of what they are doing. I was not going to get a quick answer. They explained the technical difficulties that an urban setting was going to cause and that I would need at least one repeater, two antennas of say (a long discussion among the techs on this issue), well at least twelve feet, and a very good set of walkie talkies.

After the long debate among the three of them I asked, "How much do you think this would cost? I'm not asking for a real bid, just a ballpark estimate that I can take back to my meeting." There was a long pause, and then they started rattling off numbers. "Encrypted walkie talkies will run you around $5,000 a piece, but we can get you the repeater and antennas for around $8,000. We will throw in all the hookups necessary and you should be good to go."

I understood enough to be able to convey it to those in the meeting. If I was going to be on time to meet with the Colonels, I had to get moving. As I was saying thank you and good bye, one of the techs mentioned that there was a Radio Shack right next to the Embassy in a small trailer that sat atop another trailer at the east end of the complex. They said that I should stop in there because they serviced some of the walkie-talkies that were in the Green Zone.

I did not think much of what they said other than wondering what the heck was a Radio Shack doing in Baghdad. They are taking having a store on every corner way too seriously. I ran out to where the MP's were waiting patiently and jumped into the car. They took me back to the front of the Embassy where I thanked them profusely for what they had done. It was around 1305 and I thought, "What the heck, let's go to Radio Shack".

I ran to the east side of the Embassy, just to see if the Motorola techs were just yanking my chain. Sure enough, there in the grass lawn of the Embassy stood two trailers, one stacked on top of the other. There were no red neon signs saying Radio Shack so I climbed the makeshift stairs to see what was in the upper trailer. I opened the door to the small trailer and two men were standing behind a counter as if they were at an auto parts store in Enid, Oklahoma.

"You guys sell radios here?" I said.

I am certain they had heard that line before because I got nothing.

"I just wanted to know if you are the Radio Shack here at the Embassy," I said after the long pause they had given me.

"Yep, we are the Radio Shack," one of the techs replied. They were from Enid after all.

"I heard from the Motorola guys that you do repairs on their walkie talkies. That the straight scoop?" I asked.

"You got that right. Why?" they replied.

"I am from Al Anbar Province and we had all our comm go down and for a temporary fix, we are thinking about getting some walkie talkies as a last resort. You guys think it might work for a couple of weeks?"

Both of the techs just looked at each other and smiled. I thought they were laughing at my idiotic idea. "How many you looking for?"

"Just around fifty to start to see if they are effective" I replied.

"Would 63 be OK?" said one of the techs.

"I don't follow," was all I could say.

"Lt, this is your lucky day. It just so happens that we were just packing up 63 walkie-talkies to send back to the states. We don't need them anymore and are sending them back to the Department of State."

"You guys pulling my leg? Cause if you can read the nametag, I am Lt Legge. I don't take too kindly to having the old leg pulled," I said with one hand on my nine-millimeter pistol.

"We don't mess with armed Marines," they both said at the same time. "We just got word from the Department of State that these units are to be sent home because they have been replaced by a newer unit. They all work just fine, and I am sure we could redirect them to you."

I was ecstatic. I knew that if I did not turn around and run to the conference room where the 1330 meeting was going to take place I would be late in meeting with my two Colonels, but this was just too good to be true. I had to be sure that this was for real. I asked at least a dozen questions, one being if they would throw in the chargers for free as well. I figured that while I had them in a generous mood, why the hell not? They agreed. I asked if they could confirm this within the next four minutes and they just laughed. When they saw that I was not laughing, one of them got on the phone.

Two minutes later, I had 63 walkie-talkies to take home with me. When I explained that I had to take them with me that evening, they looked to see if I was smiling and knew that I was serious. They explained to me that they had to have batteries put in them, charged to some degree, and then taken to the Motorola plant so they could synchronize them.

"Then we don't have much time to be talking now, do we?" I said. I know that I was taking complete advantage of the incredible generosity that these two men were offering, but I was now on a mission. They could see that, and they jumped on board.

By now, it was 1325 and I knew that I was in trouble, but it was well worth it. The last thing I said to the Radio Shack techs was, "If we don't pull this off, you know what they are going to do to me, don't you?" All they said was, "I think they have already done it to you." I took their statement as meaning they were going to have everything ready for me by the time I was done with my meeting.

I ran through the halls of the Embassy and got to the room where our briefing was to reconvene at around 1334. Everyone was already seated, including the two Colonels who did not have their happy faces on. As I sat down by Col Burdine he said under his breath, "Where the hell have you been Legge?" I apologized for being late and whispered to him that I had found 63 walkie-talkies that we could take back to Ramadi that evening. He just looked at me and said, "What?"

By this time the meeting had started and, as customary, Governor Ma'Moun began with his dissertation. During his twenty or thirty minutes of telling how important getting the communications fixed was, especially in Ramadi (which was where he and his two wives lived). As he was talking, I quietly told Col Burdine just a few things that I had found while we were on break. I did not want to be rude to the Governor, but in just a few quick sentences, Col Burdine got the gist of what was going on and a smile came to his face. All he whispered back to me was, "How the hell did you pull that off?"

After Governor Ma'Moun had finished his speech, the highest-ranking General felt obligated to give his little dissertation. He directed most of his speech to the two Colonels whom I worked for. He explained to them the importance of the communications, as the Governor had just done and went on to say how Al Anbar had made tremendous progress over the past couple months and had become the model of success for all the other Provinces in Iraq. To have this stall at this time simply was not an option. As the General was talking, Col Burdine had a smirk on his face. The more the General insisted on immediate action, the bigger the smirk became.

Col Brier, on the other hand, who had not heard our whispered conversation, was not smiling. This was his Province, he was in charge, and he did not want the end of his tour to be silenced by what these terrorists had done. He intently listened to the General's concerns and as the General wrapped things up on his end, he asked Col Brier what he intended to do.

"Sir, we already have plans in motion to not only solve the long range problem of permanently fixing the situation, but we also have short range plans we are working on to get things temporarily fixed," explained Col Brier.

Before he went any further, Col Burdine interrupted and said, "As a matter of fact sir, Lt Legge has some new information that will help in the situation." The look on Col Brier's face was one of, "What the hell are you interrupting me for?" But he noticed the smile on Col Burdine's face and thought it sure couldn't hurt to see what was going on. "Lt Legge, what do you have for us?" asked Col Brier.

As briefly as I could, I explained that Radio Shack had 63 walkie-talkies to be shipped back to the states and they had already received clearance to turn them over to us. I further explained that the Motorola plant had a repeater, two antennas, and all the hookup hardware we needed, and could sell them to us for roughly $8,000. I said that the walkie talkies were currently being charged, that I would take them to Motorola to be programmed, and that if all went according to plan, we could take everything to Ramadi that evening and have some communications by the next day.

Governor Ma'Moun looked over at me and gave me one of his sheepish smiles. He liked me. The commanding General just looked at me and said, "And you got all this done since our last meeting?" I replied, "Just got lucky, sir."

Col Brier just looked over at me and shook his head. This was the way a briefing should go.

CHAPTER TWENTY SEVEN

JANUARY 2006
US EMBASSY, THE GREEN ZONE, BAGHDAD, IRAQ

The meeting went on for a little longer, discussing the plans of the long range permanent repair and the importance of not only having a telecommunication system that will work well into the future, but one that had backup redundancy. If something were to go wrong, there would be a backup system. I was listening, but in the back of my mind, I was thinking of the thousand or so things I had to do in order to get this done. One of the most important things that had to be done first was getting a designated frequency for this system to operate. I had been given the name of an airman who handled all the frequencies in Iraq and luckily he was in the Embassy. I would run up to his office after the meeting.

I was then given the direct order to get this done. I mentioned in the meeting that I was not a designated PO (Purchasing Officer), which consisted of taking an hour long class on the internet explaining the importance and responsibility that went along with signing for something that the American people had to pay for. The General in charge just looked at me and said, "Son, if you can get all this crap together during a lunch break, signing for an $8,000 invoice should not be a problem." This General was used to projects that were in the million to billion-dollar range.

As the meeting came to a conclusion, I was ready to bolt. Col Brier and Col Burdine knew that there was no time to have a debriefing on the briefing. Col Burdine said, "Legge, we take off at 0300. You better have that gear ready to go." He smiled at me and I was off.

It took me a while to find the office the Air Force Tech Sergeant (TSgt). The Embassy in Baghdad is a maze of hallways and floors. I must have asked at least a dozen people where to go, each time getting closer and closer to someone who knew what they were talking about. Finally I arrived at the small cubbyhole that this particular TSgt was assigned to for his tour in Iraq. A TSgt in the Air Force is an enlisted soldier. Exactly how their rankings compared to Marine rankings is something I never did figure out, but by the amount of stripes he had on his shirt, I knew that he was not the highest ranking enlisted, but high enough that he was not going to take crap from a Lt. I would take the soft approach.

I greeted the young man cordially, explained my situation to him briefly, and asked, "So how long do you think it would take you to give us a designated frequency?"

"Around two weeks, sir," was his reply. I was expecting him to give me an answer in hours, not weeks.

"You have got to be kidding?" came out of my mouth before thinking.

"No sir," he responded. He then reached into one of the drawers in his desk and pulled out a long computer sheet. One of the old fashioned kind that had holes on each side for the archaic printer to feed it along. He showed me the hundreds of frequencies he had given out in the past six months, and then pulled out another printout, just as long, for the hundreds of new frequencies he had to designate. This is not how I wanted to start this new mission.

He had a nametag on his security badge, so I thought I would take the personal approach.

"Bob," I said in a very gentle tone even though his nametag said Robert. "I know that what I am about to ask you is going to be impossible. If lives were not at stake, I would never dream of asking you to do this, but I have my orders from about as high as it gets around here. Bob, I need this frequency by the end of the day." There was a long pause, the entire time I was looking straight into the eyes of this young man, and he eventually looked straight back at me and said, as deadpan as I have ever heard, "Can't be done."

One thing that bothers me more than anything in this world is the word "can't." I hate it in the business world, I hate it in my personal life, I refuse to hear my children use that word, and to hear someone in a war zone say "it can't be done" is just unacceptable. Nothing is impossible if you set your mind to it and don't give up. I knew I had my work cut out for me, but this TSgt was going to give me a frequency by the end of the day or he was going to have to listen to a Lt go on and on until he did.

"Bob," I started again. "Do you think our forefathers ever said, 'It can't be done?' Do you think General Washington, while crossing the Delaware river, said to his troops 'Men, this can't be done?' Bob, do you think that the Apollo astronauts, while sitting in that rocket, pointed towards the moon and turned to each other just before they lit the candle on four hundred thousand pounds of fuel (I made that number up at the spur of the moment) and said, 'Guys, I don't think this can be done?'" I went on with this obvious filibuster until the airman realized I was not going to stop until he gave me something other than, "it can't be done."

The TSgt said, "Sir, I can't promise you anything." He quickly regretted using the word "can't" in his sentence. "But I can't just take an order from a Lt who is not in my chain of command."

I replied. "Son, I will have a three star general up here in five minutes who can give you the order." I was bluffing, but I have a great poker face in a war zone. The TSgt looked at me to see if he could trace a bluff but did not want to take the chance. "I'll see what I can do," was his response.

"Bob, if you pull this off, you have the choice of either of my daughters who are of marrying age. Trust me, they are both gorgeous." If my daughters ever do read this book, if anyone in an Air Force uniform knocks on your door, I suggest you do not answer, and thank you for your contribution to this particular mission.

As I left the TSgt's cubicle, I could tell by the look in his eye he was going to pull this off. He said again that he was not promising anything, but if I came back in two hours, he would tell me if it could be done. I was already counting on it.

I raced over to the Radio Shack to see where they were on this newly developed mission that seemed to be taking on a life of its own. When I opened the door to the second story trailer, my eyes witnessed one of the most beautiful sights they had ever seen, other than the birth of my four children. There, spread out on two tables, were 63 Motorola radios sitting in their little chargers, waiting for daddy to take them to Ramadi. If I had not been in uniform, I think a tear would have formed in my eye. The two techs saw the look of satisfaction on my face and they too started to feel the importance of getting this done.

"They should be charged enough to take to Motorola in less than an hour. We took the liberty of calling the guys over there and filling them in on what to expect. They said that once you had the frequency, they would drop what they were doing and the three of them can have them done in about two hours." Now I have never said this before, and please don't get me wrong, but that is the one time in my life that I wanted to kiss a man right on the lips. I didn't, by the way.

"You guys are beyond words," was all I could say to them. "I will try and get some transportation to get them to Motorola."

"Don't worry about that. We got that covered as well. We have a pickup we can run you over with."

I looked at the walkie-talkies, looked back at the techs, and simply said,

"Thank you." The smile on their faces showed me they knew how much I appreciated what they were doing. I dashed off to do the other 998 things that had to be done to get the walkie-talkies back that night.

After an hour of making arrangements such as getting a vehicle to deliver the walkie-talkies from the Motorola plant to the helicopter-landing zone, getting the weight estimates of all the equipment we were going to be taking back, and a dozen other little things that had to be done, I headed for the TSgt's cubicle. I prayed a lot while I was in Iraq, but mainly for the well being of my family. I had an unwritten rule with God that I would not pray for military things. I knew that He was getting it from both sides and I just trusted that He would do what was right in a situation that I am sure He wishes we would not get ourselves in. But on the way to see if the frequency would come through, I have to admit, I stopped in the Chapel on the bottom floor of the Embassy and asked God for a four-digit number.

As soon as I walked into his cubicle, I knew that young TSgt had been busy and was now part of the mission. When he saw me, he immediately said, "Sir, I don't have it yet, and again, I am not making any promises, but I might have one within the hour." Again, please don't get the wrong idea, especially any single women who might be reading this book, but I hugged that young TSgt, and I am not ashamed to admit it. I was certain that he would come through.

The hug was enough for him to know that I expected that frequency in an hour, but I told him, "I am going to take the walkie talkies to the Motorola plant and I will call you in an hour."

"Sir, I can't promise you anything, but I will do my best," he said one more time trying to cover his ass just in case. But he knew that I knew that I was going to have that frequency.

I went back to the Radio Shack trailer to see where they were in getting the walkie-talkies ready to be transported to the Motorola plant. To my delight, they had already taken them to the Motorola plant. They told me that the Motorola guys had the real hard job of having to take them apart and setting them all with the new frequency. I again thanked them profusely and headed for the Motorola plant. I did not have the heart to ask them for one last favor of taking me to the plant, so I decided to hump it there. I could use the exercise and my Tech Sgt could use the time getting that frequency. All those manning the security checkpoints I had to go through remembered me from being with the MP's earlier and allowed me access to some very secured areas.

When I arrived at the Motorola plant it was plain to see that they, too, had all gotten into the spirit of the mission. The three techs had the radios spread all over the tables they had in their warehouse. Half of them were taken apart, the other half were on their way. They saw me and quickly asked, "Do you have a frequency?" I explained that we were close and should have it within the hour.

"When do you plan on taking these with you?" asked one of the techs.

"My flight leaves at 0300," was my reply.

They looked at each other and just smiled. I was again sure that these three men were not going to let me down. I checked my watch and it was getting close to the time I was to check in with the Air Force TSgt. I had made the hump over to the plant in less time than I had anticipated. At age 45, I still had a little bounce in my step.

The time had come and I asked the three techs to cross their fingers for the frequency. They did, so I made the call.

"TSgt, this is Lt Legge. Please tell me you have the frequency I need."

"Sorry sir, I don't have it." A pit started forming in my stomach. After a long pause he said, "I should have it in the next fifteen," obviously pleased with the fact that he got it done and had the opportunity to screw with me just a little.

"You're lucky I am not over there right now or you would be getting another hug and a punch."

The Motorola guys overheard the hug comment and tried not to let me hear their laughter.

Fifteen minutes later, the TSgt called the number I had left him at the Motorola plant and gave me the frequency that had been designated to the 63 walkie-talkies that I would be taking back with me. I gave the frequency to the Motorola techs, and they wasted no time jumping into getting them prepared.

"Not to put any pressure on you, but how long do you think it will take you to have everything ready?" I asked.

Without even looking up, one of them replied, "At least three hours."

I told them that sounded great and that I would get out of their hair and let them work. I had not eaten anything in at least 24 hours and I was starving. I humped back to the Embassy chow hall to get a bite to eat. Col Brier and Col Burdine were eating with General Williams when I arrived at the chow hall. I could tell they were anxious to see if we had the radios.

"Well?' was all Col Burdine could say.

"They should be ready in three hours," I said.

"That is all I wanted to hear," was his reply.

I was briefed on when the General's helicopter was scheduled to leave-three o'clock in the morning, and that we would have several Marines who could help haul all the equipment to the landing area. It was a bit of a walk to the airfield and with my estimated seven hundred pounds of gear, the trip would take a little longer than usual. I told them that I would have all the gear ready to go and in my trailer no later than 1200. They agreed on the plan and said they would show up for the equipment at 0145. I said I would be ready and dug into my hot chow. It was a great meal.

I returned to the Motorola plant three hours later only to find they had run into a bit of a snag. I don't know exactly what the problem was but it had something to do with the software that downloaded the frequencies into the radios. My hatred for computers and software was confirmed. I hate computers and they hate me right back.

"Will you have them ready tonight?" I asked.

"We have 56 of them ready to go, it is just these last seven that are acting all female," said one of the techs. For those women reading this book, don't give me a hard time, I am just repeating what I was told. I was very glad to hear that we at least had 56 ready to go and if they were not able to get the other seven ready, I was happy as a rooster in a hen house that we had gotten this far.

As two of the techs worked on those stubborn seven female radios, the other tech took me to where the rest of the equipment sat in a pile. He explained to me how the repeater worked, took everything out of their boxes and showed me how to hook everything up. We hooked up the two antennas and he explained that the higher I could get these antennas, the further these radios could reach out.

By the time I had learned as much as I could about the system I was taking back with me, the other techs had tamed the seven female radios. I signed the purchase order and they were nice enough to take me to my trailer with all my new Christmas presents. I put all the gear in my tiny trailer and saw that there was just enough room for me to lie down and get a little shut eye. I was exhausted and the two hours before the Marines would show up to grab the gear was exactly how much sleep I needed to power back up.

No sooner than my head hit the rack, I was dead asleep. I slept hard. When I finally woke up, I knew something was wrong. I knew that more than two hours had gone by. I looked at my watch and sure enough, it was 0350. I panicked and jumped out of the rack. Had I slept through Marines banging at my door? Could that even be possible?

I ran out of the trailer and went to the trailer where Bud Colby was assigned. Bud was a young 1st Lt that was General Williams' aide. He was a Naval Academy graduate and one of the finest Marines I served with. He was also a heck of a nice guy. We had been having sewage problems at the Government Center that created quite a mess and Bud arranged, through his parents back home, to get us a plumber's snake that took care of the problem. It made life at the Government center much more pleasant and much less smelly.

1ˢᵗ Lt Bud Colby (right) and LtCol Pressly.

When I got to his trailer, I banged on the door, hoping to find Bud there and that he would tell me that the helicopter had been grounded for mechanical reasons or that a dust storm was coming through. I had been stuck a few times, unable to get anywhere due to dust storms. They are an amazing sight to see. I saw a dust storm simulated in one of those Indiana Jones movies once, where a wall of dust chases after riders on horses and thought to myself, "Hollywood!" But even Hollywood understated the impressiveness of a real sand storm. They are a sight to see.

My banging received no response. This was not good. I went to the trailer where Col Burdine was assigned. No one there as well. I was beginning to get sick. I checked all the trailers where I knew were our Marines had been assigned and there was not a soul to be found. I ran to the Ops center that scheduled all flights in and out of the Green Zone only to find out that General Williams' helicopter had taken off as scheduled. I was in deep shit.

I asked when the next helicopter was heading for Ramadi. It was not until the next morning at 0200. I went back to my trailer to check one last time for faces of Marines that I recognized but did not find a one. It was time for plan B. Only problem was, I did not have a plan B.

I made a call back to my unit at the Government Center. It was still very early in the morning, but we all took shifts at night being certain that someone was awake manning the phones in case of an emergency. I thought this was an emergency. I explained to the LCpl who was on duty that I had missed the General's helicopter and to inform the XO when he woke up that I would make alternate arrangements to get the gear back to Ramadi. I would check back in as soon as I knew more.

I spent the next two hours trying to find some way back to Ramadi. I had jumped on a couple of supply convoys before, working my way around Iraq, when air transportation was impossible to find, so I thought that was my next best thing. A little more dangerous, a little longer to get to and from, but I would have rented a few camels if I could have found them.

All of my good luck had been used up on getting those radios. I blame the last ounce of luck on getting those seven female radios working. I called back to my unit to report in and was told that the XO wanted to talk to me ASAP. I waited on the phone as they went to get the XO, knowing what was coming next.

When he got on the phone, I could feel the heat coming from his red face, even though I was 90 miles away.

"Lt Legge, could you please explain to me how you managed to miss a scheduled helicopter flight?"

I tried to explain to him what had happened, but the fact of the matter was that even I was not sure what had happened. Bottom line was, I missed the frickin' flight and it was time to pay the price. I listened to the XO go on and on about how simple it was to make a simple flight and how he simply could not understand how a 1st Lt in the United States Marine Corps could not carry out a simple order such as this. The theme seemed to be simple. I was the simpleton. After sitting there and listening to him for a good five minutes, he eventually wanted some kind of response from me.

"Well Lt Legge, I talked to Lt Colby and he said that he went to your trailer several times and you were not there. What is your excuse?" was the question from the XO.

"I have none," was all I said. I had learned early on that when it came to the XO, there was no excuse that would satisfy him. After a long pause, I could tell he was waiting for me to say something else, which I was not going to do, he asked, "Well what do you plan on doing now?!"

"Sir, there is a helo leaving at 0200 that flies directly into Camp Ramadi. I will arrange with Det 2 to pick me up and take me to the Government Center," was the simple response I came up with. I could tell this made him even madder, but I was not in the mood to play any games.

"No Lt, that is not what you are going to do. You are to take the comm. equipment to Fallujah where our G6 (the head of communications) will evaluate it to determine whether it is satisfactory for what we need. You will go to Fallujah as soon as possible, and then get your ass back here as soon as you can. Do you understand that Lt Legge?"

I am not real fond of being talked down to, but I had fucked up, and that was all there was to it. I was being punished and I needed to take it like a man. I cried a little, but not in front of anyone. Not that it makes any difference, but I later talked to Lt Colby and asked him what had happened that night and he said that he had told the XO he thought he went to the wrong trailer.

CHAPTER TWENTY EIGHT

JANUARY 2006
FALLUJAH, IRAQ

I managed to get the gear to Fallujah, where the G6 had no idea why I was asking him about a set of walkie talkies that he was not going to have anything to do with. The only thing he did say was that we should just give it to the Iraqis and let them be responsible for the gear. It was a poor excuse for a band aide because it had tremendous limitations, along with dangerous ramifications if anything went wrong. We did not want to take on the consequences should anything actually go wrong. Off the record he said it was better than nothing.

I then made my way back to Ramadi on yet another helicopter flight that took me to Camp Ramadi. I was picked up by the Navy corpsman for Det 2 at 0330 that following morning and was taken to a rack that had been emptied that day because one of our Marines had been shot in the head by an Army National guardsman who had mistaken him for an insurgent during a fire fight near the traffic circle where we had repaired the tips line. The Sgt whose bunk I was to get a little shut eye in turned out to be fine. The bullet had hit him square in the middle of his helmet, and as they are designed to do, the bullet traveled along the curvature of the helmet and had only taken a little hair and scalp with it. I heard he needed a haircut anyway.

I slept through another convoy that Det 2 had going that following morning to the Government Center, because the Det 2 guys did not want to wake me. Another long conversation with the XO occurred, and I was spent. I am not much of an advocate for nervous breakdowns. My personal opinion is that they are just an excuse for not wanting to deal with things that all of us have to deal with, but that day, I have to admit, I changed my mind on the matter just a bit.

Me alongside LtCol McDonald after a very long mission.

I will not say "To make a long story short" because it is a long story, but it ended with me eventually getting the equipment to the Government Center. Gunny Pride and Gunny Jones of Det 2, Marines who had been on over two hundred convoys up and down the dangerous route Michigan, made one extra trip to take an old 1st Lt and his seven hundred pounds of gear to the Government Center. For all those Marines who made that unnecessary convoy and risked your lives…thank you.

Once back at the Government Center and having had a good ass chewing from the XO, I was ready to get this gear up and running. Gunny Daldalian , who we all called Gunny D, was not only an outstanding Marine, but a handyman by nature. He had made several of us shelves to stow our gear, something that made life much more bearable at the Government Center. It may sound trite, but having your own shelf where only your gear could be stowed, made things feel like you had your own home. Something that meant a lot to those who were far away from home.

Gunny Daldalian

I immediately tracked down Gunny D and said, "We gotta get this gear up on the roof and get it operational."

This was the kind of project Gunny D liked. He was originally from Lebanon and had little patience for those in the Middle East who were unwilling to deal with what he thought to be a problem they should be taking care of themselves. This was a project where he got to work with his hands and see the results of his work. He was not a "win the hearts and minds" kind of Marine. Little did he know what he was getting himself into.

We quickly got the gear out and worked on it in the safety of the Government Center. Going up on the roof of the Government Center was by far the most dangerous place in all of Iraq. Whatever we could do inside would lessen the amount of time we would have to spend on the roof. We gathered what little materials we had at the Government Center and began to build ourselves a communication network.

The main problem we faced was getting some kind of stand that would hold up the antennas. We made a make shift frame out of the few 2X4's we had laying around, but my gut feeling was that this was not going to work. The winds that whip through the desert are even fiercer than those that would nearly knock me down while working on a golf course in Oklahoma City while I attended the University of Oklahoma.

We got everything together and found a few volunteers who were willing to go on the rooftop and carry the gear. By the way, when it did come to asking for any volunteers to go on dangerous missions, I had to practically beat Marines back with a stick and tell them we already had enough volunteers. When it came to asking them to go outside the wire, my Marines would beg for the chance. We gathered up the gear and headed for the roof of the Government Center.

We had rehearsed several times exactly what we were going to do once on top of the Government Center. Things went like clockwork and we got the equipment up in no time. We connected everything together as I was instructed at the Motorola plant and we flipped the switch. We went back to the protection of the bottom floor of the Government Center and did our first test. I turned on a walkie-talkie, Gunny D turned on another walkie-talkie, walked down to the end of the hallway, and I pressed the key down and said "Gunny, do you read me?"

"Roger that Lt." We had communications back in Al Anbar Province. Might not be the greatest in the world, but we had communications.

Proud father of 63 Motorola Radios.

CHAPTER TWENTY NINE

JANUARY 2006
THE GOVERNMENT CENTER, RAMADI, IRAQ

We celebrated a little, but it was short lived. We tried to reach Camp Blue Diamond, where I had sent one of the walkie-talkies to see what kind of distance these radios had, but we were unable to talk to the base. Within a day, the winds of the desert did exactly what I thought they would and our antennas were lying down on the roof of the Government Center.

I called the techs at the Motorola plant in Baghdad and explained that although we had some reception with the radios, an estimated one mile radius, it was no where near the five miles we were hoping for.

"Are there any other antennas on the roof where you have our antennas?" asked the tech, obviously as distraught as I was that the system was not working.

"There are all kinds of antennas up there," I explained.

"What kind of systems are they and what frequencies are they operating?" he replied.

"I have no idea," was all I could say.

At this point I knew the conversation was going to go way over my head. The tech explained to me that if our antennas were in the middle of another system that had a stronger signal and our antennas were lower than theirs, we would be drown out with their signal. We had to go higher.

Again, there were very little building materials to work with at the Government Center, but the Gunny and I were determined to find something that we could work with to get these antennas high enough to get good reception. We stumbled across two vehicle wheels that were still connected to their separate axles. The tires were definitely heavy enough that if we cut part of the axles off, we could slide some piping we had found into the axle, secure the antennae inside the piping, and we could go just as high as we wanted to.

We also did a recon mission on top of the rooftop of the Government Center and came to the conclusion that instead of placing the antennas on the actual rooftop of the Government Center, we could place one on top of the stairwell covering that lead up to the rooftop (an additional seven feet higher than the actual rooftop level). We would be higher than anything up there. Only problem was, we would be a silhouette for all of Ramadi to see. Hell, we figured that people in Fallujah, 40 miles away would probably be able to see us. It was perfect.

We quickly constructed the brilliant idea we had come up with. Cutting the metal was not easy, but some of our junior Marines got a kick out of being told that it probably could not be done. We had an unlimited amount of plastic piping we could use to extend the twelve foot antennas as high as we wanted. The problem was two fold, how much weight could our simply constructed rig hold, and how much weight would be able to lift in order to set it in the stand we were erecting that stood almost shoulder high.

We went for a total of about 25 feet. This would surely be high enough to get up to those clean airways we so desperately needed. We secured the antennas to the piping, got the stands that our young Marines had somehow managed to cut in two, and again did our test runs within the confines of the Government Center far below the dangers of the roof top. The only problem with our dry runs were that we could not actually place the antennas in the stands we had created because our indoor roofs would not allow us to make that final step.

We were all proud of the work we had done and it was time to get all this conglomeration of spare parts up to the rooftop where it would do some good. The heaviest part, by far, was the base that the young Marines had cut. For the stairwell rooftop, we carefully, and quickly, just threw it up on the highest level of the Government Center. We placed the other unit on the other end of the rooftop. It was not as high, but the techs had told me that they did not have to be exactly the same height. We had also made a slight adjustment to how much plastic piping we had used for that antenna.

We set up the shorter antennae first. This went relatively smoothly, but the number of Marines who were breaking the horizon of the well-fortified rooftop was clearly getting the attention of the eyes that continually watched our every move. After we had the antennae in place, the Gunny and I decided to have the other Marines head back down to the safety of the lower floors. This was not just done to protect them, but to keep the two of us from being spotted readily on the stairwell rooftop.

We had already tossed the foundation for the antennae up on the eight-foot by eight foot ceiling of the stairwell so we did the same for our 25-foot antennae. We were lucky that it managed to stay on this small, flat surface. There was a small box just next to the stairwell rooftop that I used to get on top of the small perch. Once up there, all of Ramadi was visible. The electricity happened to be working at the time so the few lights that did work in the war torn city were all on. It was like seeing the skyline of New York City from the Empire State Building. It was beautiful in a way, but I quickly came to the conclusion that if I could see them, they could see me.

I called down to the Gunny, laying down as flat as I could on the concrete rooftop, that I would try and get the antennae in the base assembly we made by myself. I looked around at the fortified turrets on the rooftop where the 3/7 Marines were located and although I could not see their faces, I am certain they were either smiling at the sight of a 1st Lt on top of this stairwell, or were just flat out laughing. I stood up halfway and managed to get the base standing up. It was heavier than I thought, as I lifted it by myself for the first time.

I then grabbed the antenna that was twenty-five feet long. It was not as heavy as I was expecting. It was not light by any means, but I could lift it. I worked my way to where I had placed the base assembly and began to lift it to where I could place in the hole of the axle and get the hell of that rooftop. For those who have never tried to lift twenty five feet of antennae and piping, it is not that bad when you are just lifting it when it is horizontal to the ground, but when you try and lift it vertically, up above your waist, it somehow increases its weight at least three fold. Balancing it was another problem all together.

I managed to lift it high enough to slide into the axle only once, but my aim was not good and the weight overtook me and the antennae began to fall. There I was, three stories in the air, holding an antennae 25 feet long that weighed at least 75 pounds, on an eight foot by eight foot ledge, and the antennae and I were being taken over by Newton's law of gravity. What kept the antennae and I from falling the forty or so feet onto the concrete driveway below is beyond my comprehension. All I remember at the time is that I was not going to let go of that antenna no matter what.

I fell to the concrete of the stairwell rooftop and managed to keep the antennae with me. I laid there for a moment or two to regain my senses and strength. I was mad that I had not managed to get the antennae in the base assembly. When I regained my composure, I got to my knees, got the antennae propped straight up in the air and tried again. I rose to my feet, glanced at the skyline of Ramadi again, said a few foul four letter words, and lifted with all my strength and managed to get the antennae high enough again, but once again, could not get the antennae straight enough to fall down in the hole of the axle. I held it up longer than the previous attempt and the end of the antennae danced around the hole of the axle, teasing me that it just might fall in, but again, the antennae and I ended up on the ground. This time I had preplanned which way the antennae would fall. I decided that falling to the rooftop only 7 feet down would be better than the forty feet down to the driveway below.

The antennae got caught up in the camouflage netting we had on the rooftop and that had broken my fall as well. I managed to get it untangled and repeated the attempt to get it in the base at least two more times, but my torn rotator cuff that I had injured my first day in Iraq was not going to let me get the antennae high enough and steady enough to fall into the base assembly.

After the fourth fall, I simply stayed down. I was tired and I could just sense the snipers who took pot shots at our Marines every night were beginning to get over their laughing fits caused by some stupid Marine who was doing some sort of dance on top of the Government Center and were beginning to get sighted in on their target. I called down to Gunny D and said, "Gunny, I can't do it myself, I need some help." Gunny D, being the outstanding Marine he always had been during our tour, immediately responded, "Yes sir, right away."

I waited for Gunny D to jump up on the rooftop to help me with the antennae, but instead, I heard him running down the stairwell towards the 3/7-command center. I could not make out exactly what he said, but just recently, Gunny D came to visit me at my home in Dallas, several years after the fact, and told me that he said, "What has this crazy ass Lt got me into?"

It seemed like he was gone for an eternity as I lay there hugging the concrete rooftop, but within a minute, I could hear Gunny D running back up the stairwell. This time, I could clearly hear what he was saying. At least every other word was the F word, along with comments about Lt's and officers in general. He leaped onto the box I had used to get up to our landing, jumped up and landed practically right on top of me. I could see his eyes in the dark and all he said was, "Could we get this over with, Sir?"

We both stood up, grabbed the antennae together, lifted it up high enough to fit into the axle, and just as what had happened to me, just as we got it perpendicular to the ground and parallel to the hole we were trying to get it in, the weight seemed to triple again and we missed the hole again. We managed together to keep the antennae from actually falling to the ground, but it took a few moments to get it steadied. We both realized together that although we had not fallen to the ground, we were sitting ducks to anyone who was watching this fiasco.

"I don't know about you Gunny, but I am ready to get the hell out of here," was all I said. He responded, "Best idea I have ever heard from you, Sir." We lifted the antennae again, steadied it, and gently lowered it into the axle. Neither of us stood around to admire our handy work. I'm not sure who jumped off that landing first, but I do remember being on the rooftop floor, rolling into the stairwell, and the both of us were laughing our asses off.

I remember asking something about where the hell the Gunny had gone and he replied with some lame ass remark like he was thirsty or something, but years later on the porch of my home in Dallas, he told me he had gone down to the 3/7 Marines to find help only to get laughed at. The 3/7 Marines were the toughest sons of bitches to walk the face of the planet, but they were not stupid.

CHAPTER THIRTY

JANUARY/FEBRUARY 2006
THE GOVERNMENT CENTER, RAMADI, IRAQ

Gunny D and I went straight to our quarters where the remaining walkie-talkies were stacked in boxes. Because it was a Saturday, half of our unit had convoyed to Camp Blue Diamond for their every other weekend chance at hot chow in a chow hall and a real shower. I had given one of the radios to Col Burdine because I told him that we were going to get the system fixed. I promised that by the time he was ready to return, we would be able to talk to him at Blue Diamond, around three miles away.

We turned on one of the radios and called for anyone at 6th CAG headquarters. We only had to ask once. Loud and clear, Col Burdine barked out, "Legge, that you?" Eventually we could reach out over five miles, but there were some dead spots in the city. It was a weak band-aid, but it was a step out of the dark.

The real benefit to the whole walkie-talkie project came from something I had not really planned. Distributing the 63 radios to the Iraqis. I prepared a letter of authorization for each and every walkie talkie, stating that Achmed Khalizid had permission to be caring Motorola radio, serial number 12345678, and that Achmed was a key person in the government of Al Anbar Province. The Iraqis felt very important receiving a radio and a letter from the coalition forces that stated they were important.

Even those hard liners that clearly hated us felt important having one of these radios. Such a simple thing somehow brought us all together. I also insured all the Iraqis that this was their communication system and that we, the coalition forces, would in no way monitor it. I gave them my word. I received a little flack from some on our side who liked listening in on things, but the Iraqis knew that if I gave my word, I would not break it.

After we had the band-aid in place it was time to get the real communications up and running. For this, everything went through Baghdad. As I have stated before, I was not very fond of Baghdad. It seemed as though there was way too much talking and way too little doing in Baghdad. Thank God we don't have any place like that here in the good old USA.

Getting the plan together as to what we needed and how much it would cost was easy. Getting it approved so that we could move forward turned out to be ridiculously impossible. I ended up writing an information paper on the telecommunication repair that needed to be done in Al Anbar Province and it began like this:

INFORMATION PAPER
RAMADI SWITCH REPAIR

"The best way to describe the current atmospherics in this situation is that there are a bunch of dogs in this fight and each has an evil twin waiting for the other to make a mistake."

I cannot say any more of what was contained in the information paper because it might be considered classified and the names of the people who were involved should really remain unnamed. I doubt there are many other military information papers that began the way mine did, and although I knew I would receive resistance from those who thought my military bearing was questionable at best, I wanted to drive home a point. It was as frustrating as hell having to deal with the politics.

For every one idea, there was a group that opposed that idea. It often had nothing to do with the idea itself, just those who believed in it. I suppose every nation has its opposing factions. We have Republicans versus Democrats, Iraq has Sunnis versus Shiites, Ireland has Protestant versus Catholics. Name a country or a region and you have one group that has been raised to oppose another. In the meantime, for every week that went by not getting the communications back in order, people were dying because of it. To say that I could give a shit as to what group someone held fast with would have been a grand understatement at the time.

Some of the heel dragging had to do with money. This was true on both the Iraqi side and the coalition forces, but mainly on the Iraqi side. It turned out that the Minister of Communications in Baghdad was a Kurd princess from up north and also had financial ties to Nortel and Erickson, competitors to the Lucent technology that the Director General of Telecommunications in Al Anbar Province had chosen for the repair. Her husband had ownership in a Nortel-Erickson distributorship and would stand to make a pretty penny on selling the switches that would be necessary. It was also not a political advantage for a Kurd to help with a Sunni Province.

My time in Iraq was running out. Our unit was already transitioning with the unit that was to take our place. I worked desperately to get the communication repair done before I was to leave. I even considered extending my tour in order to get things done, but came to realize that there would always be something left undone. As a matter of fact, everything I was working on would be left undone.

Major McFadden, a major in our unit who rarely minced words put it best at the end of our tour when he told me, "Legge, I have never seen anyone work so hard on so many things and get absolutely nowhere!" He was right. There was absolutely nothing that I had worked on that had either failed to be accomplished or ended up getting destroyed in the long run.

The Tips Line was down, the Crest Program that I fought to implement was no where near being accepted, the Glass Factory I had worked on trying to get back up and running laid just as idle as when I had seen it the first day I arrived in Ramadi. There was literally no physical evidence of any success I had accomplished in Iraq.

The Glass Factory

CHAPTER THIRTY ONE

SEPTEMBER 2005 THRU APRIL 2006
THROUGHOUT IRAQ

There are so many other things that happened in Iraq during my tour. Many things happened that seemed small at the time, but in retrospect forever changed my view of the world. Some good; some bad.

There was the first time I was designated a vehicle commander in a convoy from the Government Center to Camp Blue Diamond where LCpl Thrift and I managed to jump a curb, collect at least two hundred feet of constantine wire in our axles, and leave a trail of sparks down route Michigan and into the gates of the camp. We both got a lot of laughs from our fellow Marines, but as any pilot will tell you, any landing you can walk away from is a successful landing.

The friendships I developed over a period of time with some of the brave Iraqis who were doing their best to rebuild their country is something I will treasure the rest of my life. I am almost certain that my good friend Eng Mahmood was right. I bet you anything that he and I die on the same day. I just hope that day is a long time from now and it is when Eng Mahmood and I are playing golf at the Ramadi Country Club where he and I have gotten together dozens of times over the next thirty or forty years. I hope that Governor Ma'Moun is there as well.

I once actually went to the Governor's house to set up a new computer we had for him that would allow us to have e-mail communications with him. I had to rig up a satellite dish on his rooftop in order to get reception. The Governor took my hand and guided me to where I was to install the satellite dish. It is very common to see men in the Middle East walking hand in hand. It was a great honor that the Governor had such trust in me to do that. I will admit it was a bit awkward for me, but an honor nonetheless. When we were all about to be shipped out and sent home, Governor Ma'Moun came and gave us a very touching farewell speech. Tears came to his eyes as he thanked us and wished us good fortune in the days to come. I will never forget that moment.

Farewell speech of Governor Ma'Moun.

Another interesting experience was my time as, what he called me the "attorney" for Sheik Dahir. He was the head Imam in Al Anbar Province, which is their head religious leader. His claim for damages to one of his properties had been declined and I was tasked with trying to sort it out. It may have been a questionable claim, and you can call it bribery, extortion, corruption, or anything you want, but we managed to get his claim paid. Shortly after, Sheik Dahir was instrumental in ridding violence from his province. A small price to pay.

There was also the time that I was sent to a small outpost in a hot area of Iraq where, as the Warrant Officer I worked with put it, "You ain't in Kansas no more Lt." I had a severe case of the Baghdad Bug (similar to Montezuma's' revenge but much more painful) and I grew tired of running across the courtyard where 60mm mortars often dropped in, so I just spent the night in the comfort of a porta-potty. But nobody wants to hear about that. War at its finest.

Meeting at the Government Center conference
room with Sheik Dahir (in white turbine).

Some of the events that unfolded during my tour I wish I could forget, such as the time 1st Lt "Fitz", one of the 3/7 Marines who diligently safeguarded us at the Government Center, was shot in the head. He was evacuated to Germany where his parents immediately flew, just in time to see their courageous young Marine pay the ultimate price a soldier can pay. Or the time a woman sat patiently in the lobby of the Government Center all day long to see if she was entitled to a claim for her three children who had been killed days earlier in a fire fight. Two insurgents had used children in a schoolyard to hide behind as they were attacking coalition forces. Her claim was denied. And for that poor young Marine that will never be rid of the memory of having to carry one of the little girls' mangled dead body out of harm's way.

But there is one story that stands out the most in my mind of the entire seven to eight months I spent in Iraq. It is strange to say, but there were really not many times I was angry during my tour. Certainly the constant attacks we received at the Government Center, day in and day out, irritated me. We were there to help, but for some reason there were those who did not want the citizens of Al Anbar Province to grow to trust us. But anger really never entered the equation. It would take a civilian in Baghdad to really get me mad.

My shoulder had gotten progressively worse and the medical staff at Blue Diamond had diagnosed me with a torn rotator cuff. Something I already knew. They said that I would need an MRI to be certain. The only MRI machine was in Balad, some twenty-five miles north of Baghdad. They did say, however, that I would have to be accompanied by a corpsman. Our corpsman at the Government Center had been saying throughout the tour that he wanted to see Baghdad. His family kept writing him from home, asking if he had been to Baghdad. I had an upcoming brief to give in Baghdad to tell where we were in regards to getting the communications back up in Al Anbar so I thought this would be a chance for him to see the sites and me to get a free MRI.

The trip to Balad was uneventful, but it took us two days to get there, in spite of it only being around one hundred miles away. I am not sure how many flights it took us or how many camps we sat around in, but when we finally got there we had little time to waste.

We went straight to the hospital where I was greeted by a young doctor who looked as though he had just gotten out of medical school. I explained to him what I thought the problem was, he bent my left arm and shoulder every which way he could and said, "Well Lt, looks like you have a torn rotator cuff. This is your ticket home. We just have to do a routine MRI and you can be on your way."

At first it did not really register what he had just said. I then said, "What did you say?"

"Rotator cuff tears rate you a ticket home."

It dawned on me that he was not kidding so I said, "You know Doc, you just bending my shoulder the way you did made it feel ten times better. Thanks for all your help." I turned and started heading towards the door.

"Wait a just a minute there Lt...Lt", he had forgotten my name. I kept walking as I could feel him coming after me.

"Sorry Lt, but it is my duty to make a medical judgment on your shoulder whether you like it or not."

He grabbed me by the shoulder (of course it was the bad one) and started to turn me around so that he could see the nametag that displays our last name. With a name like Legge, there couldn't be too many forty five year old 1st Lt's with the last name Legge so as he spun me around I covered my nametag with my left hand. He grabbed my wrist and gave a good solid tug to remove my hand. It did not budge. There was no way in the world I was about to leave because of a sore shoulder. I had two months left in my tour and at least five months of work to do. My shoulder had made it this far; it could make it sixty more days. He again gave a firm tug but by this time I had already made up my mind.

"Lt, I have a responsibility as a doctor."

"And I have a responsibility as a Marine."

As we stood there in a stalemate, he looked at me, I looked at him and he finally came to the conclusion that not only was I stupid, I was also heavily armed. He let go and the Corpsman and I made a hasty retreat. We headed straight for the LZ.

The trip from Balad to Baghdad is only twenty-five miles with nothing but dark desert below, but wouldn't you know it, we got fired upon. The gunners in the CH-46 helicopter both opened fire, lighting up the dark desert below and sending hundreds of rounds into sand. I have no idea if they found their mark, but by the time we got to Baghdad, I was not in a very good mood.

We got a couple hours of shuteye, and I was scheduled to meet up with Col Brier and Col Burdine to make our brief. We had around forty-five minutes before the briefing so Col Brier said he wanted to stop by and talk to one of the civilian contractors who had been sending him countless e-mails in regards to a bridge being built in Ramadi. We found his office and knocked on the door. When the contractor opened the door it looked like they had put him in some sort of closet. There was barely enough room for him in there, let alone three fully armed Marines so we conducted our meeting in the hallway.

After a few short greetings and handshakes, the contractor quickly went into his spiel. "There is a contract we started several months ago for a new bridge to be erected and the coalition forces have put a stop to it. The contract has already been approved and we are paying them $14,000 a week to do nothing. We have to get this program back on track."

Col Brier tried to explain to him that we simply did not have the troops to secure the bridge and that if it were completed, would endanger Marines who were stationed where the bridge would come into the city. In particular, the Government Center. It would be easy for a suicide bomber with a vehicle filled with explosives to ram right into the Government Center and do a heck of a lot of damage.

The contractor again said, "But we are paying $14,000 a week for this program."

Col Brier again tried to explain the danger it would cause and turned to me and said, "And there is one of the Marines who live at the Government Center who might get killed."

The contractor looked at me but was not going to change his mind. He must have said four more times that it was costing $14,000 a week, whether they worked or not. My blood was boiling. Not so much that he did not care about me, but he kept saying $14,000. First I wanted to grab him by the throat, and then ask him just what is a Marine's life worth. The conversation was going nowhere and I could tell that the two Colonels knew I was pissed, so they said they would see what they could do, just to get out of the argument.

We left and headed for our briefings. We got through the briefings and I had a few things I wanted to do before chow, like one last time thank all those involved in getting the radios together. By the time it was ready to have dinner chow, I had calmed down and steam was no longer coming out my ears. I began to walk to the chow hall and across the street was the contractor. I pretended I did not notice him and picked up my pace.

From across the street I heard, "Lt Legge." I ignored the call and kept walking. Again came the call, "Lt Legge." By this time he was crossing the street to come after me. I could tell there was no way I could avoid this meeting, so I stopped, turned towards him and tried to give him a civil smile.

He reached out to shake my hand, which I did in return. His handshake was surprisingly firm. I had not expected that.

"Lt, I know that you wanted to pull out that nine millimeter pistol of yours earlier today and put a round through my eyes, but you have to understand that this is my job whether I like it or not. We simply cannot let them stop us from moving forward and it will also provide hundreds of jobs for men who would otherwise be making the money to feed their families by shooting at you guys."

I was shocked that he had thought about the fact that that was one of our main objectives and was impressed that he was even thinking along those lines. I simmered down and said, "I did not want to put a round between your eyes."

"Don't bullshit me Lt. I know when a Marine is ready to kill. I wore one of those uniforms for twenty two years." Holy shit, this guy was a Marine. Now that really shocked me. I mellowed even further and said, "I can appreciate your job and the decisions you have to make; it is just that that bridge would really put some Marines in a bad spot."

"I know, and you are one of them," he said with his voice becoming a bit strained.

"It's not so much me. I am sure you have gathered that I am no spring chicken, but we have some awfully good young Marines at the Government Center who do a heck of a job protecting this old Marine. If anything were to happen to them I just could not bear the thought."

He said, "I know, I have two sons in the Marines and one of them is in Ramadi." His eyes were now looking down at the ground and were beginning to fill with tears. I stood there not knowing what to say. How could a man like this have to make decisions that might cost the life of one of his own sons? All I said was, "You build that bridge. We will take care of the rest."

I patted him on the shoulder and did not wait for a reply. He was with his sons in his thoughts and prayers. So the next time you are talking bad about politicians, or hating those in cultures that are not like your own, remember that man who had to make the decisions that I don't think you and I will ever have to make, and remember as well, there is no black or white.

CHAPTER THIRTY TWO

APRIL 2006
GRAPEVINE, TEXAS

Returning from Iraq is still a bit of a blur. We flew into Kuwait and waited several days until our flight was ready to take off after many delays. My daughter Amber went into labor with my first grandchild. Gracie was born five minutes before I boarded the plane to return home.

Me in Kuwait minutes before departure and
the birth of my first grandchild.

When I got back to the states, we still had to go through debriefings and medical evaluations before we were to be set free among civilians again. I was then bussed to Charlotte, where the adventure had begun, went through a ceremonial welcome home at the units' headquarters, and then jumped on a plane back to Dallas.

I was anxious to get to my house with my children, and to my own bed, but I knew that there were many family members and friends who wanted to greet me at the airport. When I arrived, there was a news crew and all of my family and friends there to greet me. I only remember a few things about the arrival. One was that the revolving door was stuck that lead to the baggage claim where everyone was congregated. The second was my daughter in a wheel chair with my brand new grand daughter in her arms. The film crew was struggling to get a shot of the returning grandfather from Iraq, but they disappeared from my mind as I was hugging my children and Gracie. The rest is just a blur3

I knew that everyone wanted to talk to me and welcome me home so I had made arrangements to go to the Joe's Crab Shack just outside DFW airport in Grapevine. Every night that I was in the Government Center in Ramadi Iraq, before I would hit the rack for much needed sleep, I would go to the back door of our building where just outside we had built a small bunker where we were allowed to smoke. I hate the fact that I smoked over there, but it was a time I used to relax and transport myself back to my home where my children would laugh and play. There was a special spot at that Joe's Crab Shack, outside near the playground they had built that I would imagine I was each night. It was a very specific spot. I would imagine that I was leaning up against the railing, with a glass of wine, watching my children play on the slides and swings. It was not just a memory I was in, it was if I was actually there. There was even a plant in a pot between next to a pole that I would lean up against as I watched my children. Those many, many nights I was at the Government Center, thinking of being home, I could actually feel that plant brushing up against my Marine Corps uniform. It was the only time I afforded myself the luxury of thinking about home. The rest of the day was spent concentrating on what was at hand.

When we got to Joe's Crab Shack from the airport, we were seated inside where we all ordered our food, but I wanted to go watch my son play in the play area. I took my wine outside and went to the spot I had spent so many nights pretending I was these past eight months to watch the children play. I stood in the very spot that I had imagined to be so many nights. It was so nice to be home, but even though I had not actually been in that spot for over a year, something was missing. The plant that I had brushed up against so many times was gone. It did not feel the same.

I have been back to that Joe's Crab Shack at least a hundred times since I have been home. Each time, without fail, after we have eaten our dinner, I still go to that spot. It is a place that I consider to be my spot. I do miss the plant, however, but I have come to know that things change. We just can't avoid that.

BACKWARDS

This is the part where I give my opinions as to what I think we accomplished in Iraq. Since I have a forward to this book I thought it deserved a backwards. Let me first state that my opinion, just as anyone else's opinion, is worth 1 out of 6,400,000,000. There are 6.4 billion people in this world, each with an opinion. Each equally valid. Each carries the same weight. I could honestly care less if you are in agreement with my opinions. If you stop here, at least keep these stories in mind in coming to a conclusion as to whether what we did in Iraq was worthwhile or not.

Let me first say, with absolutely no reservation what so ever, what we did in taking Saddam Hussein, and especially his sons, out of power was an absolute necessity. I refuse to get into an argument with anyone about weapons of mass destruction or about Iraq's involvement with 9/11. That to me misses the point. I think the pro-active measures that President Bush and Prime Minister Tony Blair took back then was not only necessary but incredibly brave of them. They had nothing to gain because I am certain they knew they would be bombarded by Monday morning quarterbacks.

But my opinion, the Presidents, or the Former Prime Ministers is not important. I worked with many, many Iraqis who were not only part of his regime, but in some cases were direct associates of Saddam. Although very few Iraqis will publically thank the coalition forces for taking him out of power, there is not a single person in that region, from any country, who deep down does not feel a sigh of relief that he is gone. The atrocities that Saddam committed on his enemies, and even his own people, are countless. The inhuman acts that his sons, especially Udah, perpetrated on their own "people" is beyond belief.

I came to know many of those who had family members who had either been raped or killed for no reason by these madmen. At first they were unable to speak of these acts. After time and growing to trust me, in confidence, I was told some of what happened under the reign of Sadam and his sons. If there is anyone in this world that would like to take their side and have a private "discussion" with me as to having them removed, bring it on. I am sure there are also people out there who would defend Hitler's atrocities as well

This is not to say that "we" are completely right. Any time violence is resorted to, no one is completely in the right. One thing that I actually admire about those countries in the Middle East is how the common man deals with injustice or crime. They have a much lower rate of violent acts than the United States does. I once read a study on violent acts committed from country to country and was shocked as to the results. When it came to the amount of violent crimes that the average American suffered per thousand, it was around 300 for every thousand, compared to around 12 per thousand in most other countries.

This is just an average of crimes such as rape, murder, armored robbery and the like, but it is a telling tale. I have also been in arguments with those that completely defend our country stating things such as that other country simply does not report such crimes, especially those against women. Again, I have no desire to argue. Anyone can make a case on any group of facts they chose to review. The point is, we too have our problems with violence, just as any other country.

I believe that every country has its own right to follow their own beliefs, whether the rest of the world agrees with their ways or not. It is also up to the people of each country to make the changes amongst themselves to improve what they deem to be necessary. Although I believe in the morality and foundation that America is based on, I do not believe it is our destiny or right to impose those on others.

What I do believe, however, is if any country or people choose to leave their borders and invade ours or those we are friends with, you had better take heed. It has become a time where technology has grown to where you can now do far too much damage to too many to allow you to go unchecked. We, and I mean the general consensus of the world, will no longer tolerate it. I am afraid that there will be one more catastrophic event that will cement us together, but we will stick together.

History is not made in a day. It is not made in a year. History is a look back on an era. The era we are in is the era of what direction we choose to go. Seeing the tolerance and restraint that the majority of the soldiers I had the privilege to serve with makes me proud. We came to a cross roads of increased violence and force to that of restraint. We choose restraint. Whether anyone agrees with that or not, I have seen it with my own eyes. I think history will bare that out.

As to my personal contribution on what transpired, there really is nothing tangible to point to. But there are people I have met that I have touched and they have touched me. People who may have once considered me to be the enemy now may not be friends, but are no longer enemies. The physical things that we did together can be destroyed with the blast of a bomb or the scorching of a fire, but the effort we did together can never be taken away.

The most common question I have been asked upon returning from Iraq has been "Was it worth it?" I have pondered that question a lot. It is a year that I will never get back from being away from my family. Some of the physical and mental tolls that the war inflicted on me and everyone I served with will remain with us for the rest of our lives. My children tell me I am not the same. I know that and wish it were not so, but there is one thing that no one can ever take away from me. One thing that was measurable, according to those who took measurements.

The Tips Line that the Iraqis' and I repaired was said to have saved a Marine a week and countless Iraqi lives. For the Iraqis lives saved, I give full credit to Hamad. The Tips Line was up for only sixteen weeks while I was over there. It might not seem like much, but every Christmas morning since I have returned, I think of the sixteen families who get to celebrate with their Marine. There is no way to know who those families are or even how happy they might be, but they are there. Each Christmas morning, I smile for those unidentified families.

For the families that celebrate their Christmas' without the Marine they sent over to help, believe it or not, I smile for them as well. That may sound odd or even callous in a way, but I know that these Marines are still doing what they were so well trained to do. They are protecting those who need protecting. Only these Marines now protect those far more important than those of us down here.

Major Chelkowski and "Chi Guy" who brought us tea every day. He hated us when we arrived. He hated us a little less when we left. Major accomplishment.

Governor Ma'Moun at his desk in his office.

Convoy preparing to leave Camp Blue Diamond.

Me sitting at the Governor's desk.

School filled with girls in Fallujah.

Me next to a Marine that clearly needed to shave.

Engineer Mahmood and me planning our next telecommunications repair.

"Chi Guy" looking just happy to be there.

Me doing my "Dust Pan Man' duties.

Taking a break in the Iraqi head where I always had reserve seating.

Oliver North came to the Government Center just to say hello,

On my way to becoming the Ping-Pong champion of
Ramadi on our make shift Ping-Pong table.

Typical day waiting on Iraqis for a meeting.

In the lobby of the Government Center where I asked this
young Iraqi girl why she thought the Marines had come
to Iraq and it unbroken English replied "The oil."

Inside the US Embassy in Baghdad

While at the Embassy hard decisions had to be made.

Picture of Det 1 just before departure to Iraq

Me in my gear (you can't go anywhere into battle without your laptop)

Fiber-Optic crew making the repairs, despite
knowing we were receiving sniper fire.

The Calendar wall we made counting down the days of our tour.

Twenty seconds after I finished my Thanksgiving meal.

At the Marine Corps Ball in Washington DC with my date.

Behind the Embassy in Baghdad where a collection of
statutes of Saddam were no longer on display.